Employee Engagement & Communication Research

For Ken

Best wishes

Susan Walker

17/ Nv 2012

Employee Engagement & Communication Research

Measurement, Strategy & Action

Susan Walker

KoganPage

LONDON PHILADELPHIA NEW DELHI

First published in Great Britain and the United States in 2012 by Kogan Page Limited

120 Pentonville Road	1518 Walnut Street, Suite 1100	4737/23 Ansari Road
London N1 9JN	Philadelphia PA 19102	Daryaganj
United Kingdom	USA	New Delhi 110002
		India

www.koganpage.com

© Susan Walker, 2012

The right of Susan Walker to be identified as the author of this work has been asserted by her in accordance with the Copyright, Designs and Patents Act 1988.

ISBN-13: 978 0 7494 6682 4
E-ISBN: 978 0 7494 6683 1

British Library Cataloguing-in-Publication Data

A CIP record for this book is available from the British Library.

Library of Congress Cataloging-in-Publication Data

Walker, Susan.
    Employee engagement and communication research : measurement, strategy, and action / Susan Walker. – 1st ed.
        p. cm.
    ISBN 978-0-7494-6682-4 – ISBN 978-0-7494-6683-1   1. Employee motivation–Research.
2. Communication in organizations–Research.   3. Organizational change–Research.
I. Title.
    HF5549.5.M63W3475 2012
    658.3'14–dc23

                                                                                    2012019428

Typeset by AMNET
Printed and bound in India by Replika Press Pvt Ltd

Remembering my parents
Lawrence and Valerie, with gratitude

CONTENTS

11   Turning the results into the organizational story   137

12   An international perspective   149

13   Making the business case   157

PART 3: Implementation   167

14   Lights… Sound… Action!   169

15   The six key stages   173

16   Putting the action plan in place   185

ACKNOWLEDGEMENTS

My first thanks must go to Sir Robert Worcester who was brave enough to ask a right-brained communicator to join his research firm MORI. Also to his colleague Roger Stubbs for his equally brave attempts to awaken the left brain to help me understand the complexities of research.

Acknowledgements and sincere thanks go to all those whose names appear in these pages, having contributed their expertise and experience in the form of conversations, case studies and comments to this book. Although it may be invidious to name one among so many helpful friends and colleagues, I should give special thanks to statistician Ken Baker for his patience while we steered a course between accuracy and simplicity.

My former MORI colleagues Lyn Roseaman and Neil Barber checked out research sections while IABC colleagues Gloria Walker, Ezri Carlbach and Sam Berrisford gave me the benefit of their counsel.

I should also thank my friend Kathleen Waton for her support and confidence and Jonathan Walker for his practical advice.

Most of all I must record my appreciation of my husband Tim Barrett without whose patience and encouragement during the gestation of this book, it would not have been completed.

Introduction
Energizing research for high performance

The annual employee survey is dead.
Discuss.

A groundswell of opinion questions traditional approaches, asking if these continue to meet the needs of today's business world. Tough economic conditions, global competition, pressures on costs and profitability are changing the world of work.

The good news is that some stars in the engagement and communication research world show that it is alive and thriving: organizations with effective internal research programmes contributing to their business success and professionals in consultancies and elsewhere pushing the boundaries with fresh ideas and approaches, which they share with us in this book. These stars believe that internal research can play an active role in organizational issues to create:

- employee high performance for business success;
- recruitment, motivation and retention of the most talented people;
- a relationship of trust between the organization and its people;
- knowledge sharing, best practice and innovation;
- employee engagement, especially during tough times with downsizing, pay freezes and benefits reductions;
- return on the investment in engagement and communication systems and initiatives;

- the growing expectations – and determination – of employees to have a voice in their organization and see action implemented from research.

For other organizations the situation is very different. Fewer than one in five employees strongly believe that survey results will be acted upon, according to Aon Hewitt's European Engagement database. Their manager survey found that only 40 per cent of managers spend more than five days a year on engagement survey activities. Feedback suggests that these figures are no better elsewhere in the world.

How does this happen? Why does measurement not measure up? Where is the action to address issues and help build the business? What stops the inspiration, innovation and imagination to move internal research forward?

Here are some common barriers:

Safe and sorry: entrenched in tracking over time, these research programmes dare not change content or approach. The survey 'owners' here are sorry, but they would rather be safe.

Norm again: excessive adherence to standard norm questions can preclude relevant upcoming issues specific to that particular organization.

Miracle seekers: these believe that a few standard set questions can bring all the answers they need.

Process-project driven: here the research becomes a repeat 'project', often in the hands of administrators rather than decision makers. So this is their focus – and, like safe and sorry colleagues, nothing new is developed.

The end: the results should not draw a line under the research, so lack of action undermines all that has gone before. Interpretation, understanding insights contributing to business improvements should come next – it's the start, not the end.

So what of the future? Can these barriers ever be overcome? As an optimist I hope – and think – so. And this is the inspiration for this book, which answers these key questions:

Face forward: some of the terms such as 'measurement' suggest past and present experiences and opinions. Why not focus more on a way forward for the future to stimulate high performance and engagement?

People power: communication is no longer solely in the ownership of the organization. People have access to social media. Are you looking at what your people are saying in the blogosphere and employee-generated websites?

Inclusive world: instead of focusing on the individual as a worker, let's look at them as a whole – people with enthusiasms, as parents, community activists? What about personality type questions to see if profiles align with what the organization needs?

Below the surface: typical measurement skims the surface of a wide subject range. Why not specific surveys about performance, communication, personal development, innovation, customer service, where each deserves separate depth measurement?

Opportunities: a frequent complaint is the unreasonable number of requests for question inclusion. A threat – or an opportunity? Why not a monthly internal 'omnibus' survey with different questions owned by different functions combined into one overall survey?

Segmentation: again taking the lead from our marketing colleagues, why not look at profiling our audience beyond the usual demographics of age, service length, department, etc?

Methodology: as more people have online access, feedback will become faster. Are you keeping up-to-date with new methods and keeping an eye on potential feedback from social media platforms, phone-in and texting?

Heart of the organization: does the research truly reflect the strategy, mission, values and culture so it can become an integral part of the business and contribute to organizational success?

Look upon this book as a gateway. Many of the subjects merit – and indeed have – specialist books of their own. As a gateway, it opens the door to internal research and points the way to learning more for those who want to follow that path.

First let's define what makes research among employees different from other research. There are four main factors:

- The audience may have a varied profile, but is one community with common interests.

- Deep understanding of the individual organization, its business, market, culture and people is essential.

- Its purpose is not just to listen but also interpret, give feedback and develop ways to bring active improvements.

- There is no end point: it can, and should, form a continuing close relationship with all in the organization.

If you are already involved with such research or planning to do so, this book will guide you, whether it is the full-scale employee survey or research focusing on a particular subject such as communication, engagement, change, mergers or corporate social responsibility. You might be:

- Managing a research project commissioned from a specialist research organization: this will give you the understanding and knowledge to select the partner that is right for you and work alongside them effectively.

- Carrying out your own research internally from the human resources, communication, engagement, change, customer-service viewpoint.
- Already in the research field, either internally or with an agency but want to know more about the specialist employee side.
- A people manager interested in listening and responding to feedback from your team.
- With a consultancy where you need to know what such research can offer to advise clients on their best options.
- In the private sector for a large or small organization.
- In the public, government, charity or not-for-profit sectors. The term 'organization' here refers to any type of business or agency, while 'board' encompasses trustees and other not-for-profit stakeholders.
- In any country or have global responsibilities. Many examples come from the UK as that is where I am based, but the messages are often as relevant internationally.

There's a well-known saying: what doesn't get measured doesn't get done. So it is no surprise that communicators, human resource and change managers and other professionals recognize the need to measure and evaluate their work, particularly its worth to their organization, and seek the most effective ways to achieve this.

To respond to those needs, this book takes you through three essential stages:

- Our first measurement basics section provides an introduction for tools to build a firm foundation, ensuring the outcomes are robust and reliable.
- Our strategic section looks at how to align the research with the business and show senior management it has a real role within your organization to drive engagement and high performance.
- Our third section, action implementation, covers the all-important stage of feedback, addressing emerging issues and planning to bring improvements.

Throughout the book, conversations with top professionals in their field and case studies of successful research programmes share their experiences with you to show how their investment was worthwhile to the business.

What about the innovation and inspiration? You will find ideas to stimulate your own thinking here. As an entrance, the book also gives access to other resources you may find useful: websites of those contributing or quoted are given in the appendices so you can keep up-to-date with the latest thinking from that expert while suggested templates are also provided as well as sources for more information.

Changes to the business environment and technology advances will always extend and enhance research among employees, adding new perspectives with conversations, comment and consultation broadening its borders. So the best advice is to keep your feet firmly on the ground by learning about the best tools and techniques available today but also to continually look towards the horizon at emerging opportunities to add to the evolving field of internal research.

What's in a word? Internal research is sometimes called measurement (quantity/volume), audit (review, inspection), evaluation (assessment, valuation), analytics (diagnostics using data), or employee survey (usually the all-company research programme.) Whatever the description, the basic tools and approach are similar and here 'internal' or 'workforce' research is used to cover all these terms.

Conversation 1
In the beginning – a conversation with **Sir Robert Worcester**, pioneer of employee research

As the best-known pollster in Britain, Sir Robert Worcester, founder of Market & Opinion Research International (MORI), is often quoted in the media. However, he may be less well-recognized as pioneer of a branch of research that rarely hits the headlines: employee surveys.

Sir Robert first joined the research field with Opinion Research Corporation in Princeton, New Jersey, USA. When he came to the UK in 1969, he arrived with three great research passions: corporate image, financial and employee. In this he was prescient. It soon became clear that the success of a business in terms of these three is closely linked: financial performance with corporate image, which in turn relates to those who contribute to both – the employees.

When Sir Robert founded MORI, why did he pioneer employee surveys as an integral part of his business? 'There was virtually no such research then,' he explains. 'Some studies looked at the company newspaper – but no real attention [was] paid to wider issues like upward communication. I felt that employee surveys had the potential to do good in the workplace – it was an opportunity for employees to come up with ideas and suggestions and to tell the boss what they really thought – sometimes for the first time.'

Early experience showed that bringing market research techniques to create effective employee surveys was not enough – the commitment and interest of the 'boss' was an essential ingredient. 'Our first large-scale survey was for Barclays, which then employed 54 thousand people … its success was largely due to the fact we had full co-operation from the chairman and the personnel director throughout.' So one of Sir Robert's key advice points before embarking on employee research is to ensure that senior management is fully engaged. He also quotes the example of another early MORI survey about the Five Principles of the Mars Company: 'It was clear from the outset that the two owners, John and Forrest Mars, would be personally involved in every stage of the project – this proved integral to producing feedback which helped to bring the principles alive throughout the business.'

What does Sir Robert see as the main pitfalls threatening the success of employee research? 'Don't assume that you know what the results will be,' he says. To avoid this preconception, he introduced his 'guesstimate' – a short prediction questionnaire:

The best way to stop senior management claiming that they knew what the outcomes would be all along, is to ask them to predict what the figures will be for certain questions. The key figures from the guesstimate are the high and low figures, revealing how very different the perceptions are around the board table as well as their combined scores showing that as a group overall they are over optimistic or even in certain cases pessimistic.'

Some senior management teams have a not-invented-here attitude – I came across this in one large blue chip organization where managers had some firm views, refusing to listen to our professional advice and after one meeting it was clear that it would be impossible to continue – I was not prepared to compromise our principles for anyone.

A fundamental requirement of Sir Robert's before embarking on a survey is for the organization to agree to communicate the results honestly to employees. Has he ever met with a refusal? 'Yes, just once. It was a well-known media company – they would not commit to publishing the results so I told them straight: MORI would not carry out their survey.'

He does appreciate that senior management may fear hearing about aspects that they simply will not be able to address. 'But I never advocate management by opinion poll,' explains Sir Robert:

If the workforce believes that a particular benefit is poor, and it is poor, the company must improve that benefit – or explain clearly why that is not possible – or live with the consequences. But if, objectively, that benefit is wonderful but considered poor – a misconception – then a communication programme needs to correct that false impression.

In Sir Robert's career he has met – and overcome – many research challenges. However, there is one type of research that, as he says, no investment can buy. That is the research which should have been done in the past. 'You would be surprised at the clients who have asked for research into a campaign or initiative to see how effective it has been – but there is no "before" baseline to work from,' he says. So further counsel from Sir Robert is to plan ahead and ensure that the relevant research has been undertaken so that the impact of any programme or project can be accurately assessed.

Back in 1973 in an address to a Market Research Society Conference Sir Robert asked: 'Who can tell what good will flow from systematic, objective measurement of employee attitudes to help better decision making. We can only hope that over the next years we shall find out.' The fact that listening to employees, in a developing number of ways as described in this book is now recognized as an integral part of creating a successful business is his answer.

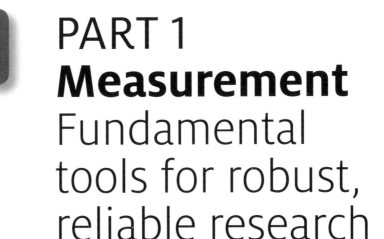

PART 1
Measurement
Fundamental
tools for robust,
reliable research

Defining your objectives

01

This chapter sets the scene for clear objectives and approach for your project, looking at the why, who, where, when, what and how as part of the decisions to be made before proceeding.

Any research project – whether small or large – sets out on a journey. It usually starts with the notion that some form of measurement will be a good idea, either a new project or repeat of a regular study which continues through the process until its destination, when any issues raised will, it is hoped, be addressed.

Most journeys begin with the best of intentions. But if you are not sure about where you are going, there's a strong possibility of getting lost along the way and arriving at the wrong destination. So firstly, draw up a clear direction in the form of a clear strategy and mission for your project from the start.

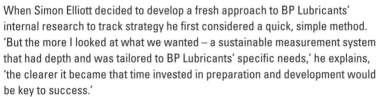

CASE STUDY 1 BP Lubricants: preparation is the key

When Simon Elliott decided to develop a fresh approach to BP Lubricants' internal research to track strategy he first considered a quick, simple method. 'But the more I looked at what we wanted – a sustainable measurement system that had depth and was tailored to BP Lubricants' specific needs,' he explains, 'the clearer it became that time invested in preparation and development would be key to success.'

To achieve this, Simon brought in independent consultant Helen Coley-Smith, who contributed valuable strategic input. 'First essential was to tie in with the business,' says Helen. 'Any measurement system had to demonstrate value, gain cultural acceptance in a global business and develop into a reliable tracking tool – not a one-off intervention.'

The first steps took twin paths: one internal, to fully understand how measurement could contribute to the needs of the business and the second external, to review the work already undertaken to determine the contribution of communication and engagement to business performance.

Simon and Helen looked at a range of research reports such as Towers Watson, IABC, Gallup and the Future Foundation. The Sears model (see Chapter 13) was particularly influential in their thinking.

At the same time, BP Lubricants' 'winning formula' strategy needed clarity and meaning for employees so they could contribute to business goals. The external research proved useful but it was clear that a performance management approach specific to their business was needed. 'I found it helpful to think about what should be in the final presentation at the end of the project – the information that the leadership team would want relating to business performance,' explains Simon. 'This gave us a goal to work towards and a clear direction to our thinking.'

Thus the next step was to establish a firm link between the measurement and Lubricants' business strategy by relating communication and engagement interventions to practical business issues such as organization focus, customers and growth. 'This became our communication and engagement value tree,' adds Helen. 'We found this made the important conversations with others in the business much easier as they were able to recognize the connection between these activities and business success.'

Now the thinking needed to be transformed into a measurement process that was, in Simon's words: relevant, pure and simple. This resulted in six clear measures covering the relationship between Lubricants' communication and engagement activities (inputs) and what employees think and feel (outputs). Under inputs are:

- Communication effectiveness.

- Engagement effectiveness.

And under outputs:

- Awareness and understanding (mainly about business strategy).

- Commitment to making the strategy a success.

- Confidence in leadership and future of the business.

- Trust in leadership and the strategy.

These then were the six key measures (key performance indicators, KPIs) of the research programme. Questions were developed to flesh out each KPI, each with a clearly defined purpose. 'We realized how important the visual aspect would be,' emphasizes Helen. 'The leadership team would soon be bored by a set of the usual PowerPoint slides – we needed to present results in a clear compelling way.' Using the KPIs, a communication 'dashboard' was developed that took the positive scores from the questions under each of the six headings to give an at-a-glance view of the business. This gave an initial overview that could also be used to summarize the results for different parts of the organization. With 17,500 employees across 60-plus countries involving 17 languages, this made a potentially complex task much easier to administer.

FIGURE 1.1   Communication and engagement dashboard

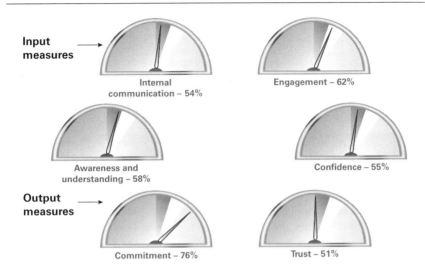

Input measures →

Internal communication – 54%

Engagement – 62%

Awareness and understanding – 58%

Confidence – 55%

Output measures →

Commitment – 76%

Trust – 51%

The success of this model for performance managing communication and engagement has become clear over the years providing input and insights for action. From initial planning to completion of the first measurement programme, took well over a year. Development of the thinking lasted several months but this was time well spent according to Simon: 'I realized that previous research at Lubricants had not been strong enough to be sustainable – it lacked rigour. So I thought – now let's crack it. Yes, development of our model took time, energy and effort but it resulted in a complete picture of communication and engagement activity as a strategic driver of business value.' So based on their experience, what advice would Simon and Helen give to others embarking on a similar venture? 'Preparation and planning is paramount,' they agree.

Some organizations move directly to thinking about the 'how' to carry out the research and forget the five 'Ws'. Don't make that mistake. Ask these questions.

- **Why** is this research essential to our organization's success?
- **Who** owns the research and do others need to be involved to ensure that the research meets the needs from a business/public value viewpoint?
- **Where** should that research be carried out: focused on a specific area/ function or is it needed throughout our whole organization?
- **When** will be the best time to ensure that the management information gained can be fed effectively into our planning processes?
- **What** is the purpose? Is it intended (as some used to say) as a general temperature check or level of engagement? Or are we concentrating on

a specific activity or initiative? Or do we want to look more widely, at beliefs and behaviours linked with business success? Or are we falling into the trap of saying: 'We have always done an annual survey?'

Why do many research projects fall into that last snare: the sacred cow of the annual employee survey? This can lumber along faithfully year after year without question and little change. It is this stagnant approach that gives a bad name to the whole area of internal research.

Examples of stagnancy and the annual employee survey

A survey had been in progress for several years in one large financial retail organization with UK-wide branches. The short questionnaire, which focused very much on human resource issues, had not changed or been revised at all during that time. However, the business scene had changed radically with staff expected to become more proactive in selling. There was also an increasing focus on customer service, which was becoming higher on the senior management agenda but notably absent from the survey coverage which had become increasingly irrelevant. A suggestion to the communication manager responsible for the research to review and revise the questionnaire fell on deaf ears. **'The CEO is pleased with the high response rate,'** he explained. **'So I don't want any changes which might reduce that.'**

A food retailer had a similar long-standing questionnaire that did not include up-to-date business issues such as understanding of the strategy and future direction. Why no change there? The explanation this time was that managers' bonuses were based on their results and any alterations might raise suspicions that **the underlying purpose was to reduce those bonuses rather than improve the value of the research**.

Such reactions do nothing to create a survey that is an integral, vibrant part of business life. Tracking questions over time has value to measure progress, but should not outweigh the potential worth of the overall project.

My suggestion would be to start with a blank sheet – relatively easy if this is your first survey but more difficult if a research programme has been running for some time and tracking progress might be lost with substantive changes. So go back to first principles to define the purpose of the measurement. Thinking of Sir Robert Worcester's earlier comments about the close involvement of the leadership in his early surveys, I wonder how many internal research projects nowadays have input from the top at the outset?

- Have you asked your own leadership what they want from their people to help the business move forward? This should be the bedrock of any research among employees generally, about communication, engagement or change. How many times does the leadership team only know about what is being surveyed when they are presented with the results? Too late for any meaningful input from the people who are planning and directing their organization's future. So this is the time to be assertive – and if the senior team do not want to know then look at Chapter 13, which gives evidence of the linkage between employee engagement and communication and business success. If this has no effect, ask yourself is there any point in carrying out the research?

- Define what the research will add to the business in practical terms. This is a perfect opportunity to set clear objectives and targets. Other functions usually have clear directions – why not the internal research programme?

- Get to know the overall strategic plan and those of the various functions and translate these into practical points to which employees could contribute or influence. These will help you formulate the approach and content for the research.

- Based on this input, envisage what the final presentation might look like. Of course you will not have the actual figures, but why not draw up an outline of what information and guidance you would like to be able to give to senior management and others? It is not too early to start thinking about the outcomes.

Who has the responsibility for the internal research? In some cases it is owned by the internal communication function (whether it is communication measurement or a more general change or engagement survey). In others it may be the change team or other specialist function such as the market research or insight unit. But perhaps the most frequent owner is the human resource function. In many cases, the HR team does an excellent job but there are instances of this department holding the project so close that other input is excluded from other functions that could add value to the process. This means that coverage focuses on human resource issues – important though they are – while business issues such as customer service and communication are secondary or omitted completely.

My view is that responsibility should be shared with internal communications as the study itself is a communication channel. However, whoever owns the project, collaboration with other functions is essential.

- Contact departments such as customer satisfaction, public relations, brand management, financial and support functions as well as internal communications, change and human resources.

- Extensive consultation risks excessive input so this should not be an open door to a wide range of disparate questions but carried out within clear, distinct guidelines.

Where that research should be carried out is another key question to consider. The usual approach is to ask everybody everything but is this the most productive approach? Are there specific functions or topics that would benefit from closer focus?

- People in front-line jobs may have particular insights into customer service to contribute that could bring improvements. Certainly their attitudes and behaviours form a vital part of good service.

One misconception revealed by research comes from a retailer. Questioned what should be done when stacking shelves and asked by a customer about a particular product, most staff said they would just point in the direction of where it was in the store. In fact, they were supposed to take the customer personally to the spot but local managers were not enforcing this. Here was an immediate opportunity to improve customer service. Next time you enquire and are taken politely to where you will find the product, you will see that desired behaviour in action.

- New recruits tend – naturally – to be more positive about their organization. Research studies in many organizations reveal there seems to be a two year 'itch'. At that point employees decide to stay or leave, often wasting investment in induction and training. So why not sample recruits every few months to identify the tipping point when enthusiasm fades and they become disengaged so this can be addressed? A good example of this follows in our case study about enthusing new recruits.

CASE STUDY 2 Keeping new recruits' enthusiasm alive in Virgin Atlantic

When people first join an organization it is usually with a spirit of enthusiasm and anticipation. However, service length analysis for employee research often shows a dip within a couple of years' service. Then the disappointed leave, wasting both recruitment and training costs. How many organizations look at the reasons behind jobs not living up to expectations in a special project?

An exception brave enough to do so was Virgin Atlantic, experiencing above average attrition rates some years ago among cabin crew staff during their first year of service. This was a costly issue, given the investment made on an ongoing basis in the recruitment, training and retention of new staff in this key customer-facing role. It was imperative to understand what was going wrong and to put in place relevant interventions to help turn the tide of leavers. This was the challenge for Karen Wisdom (then with the research firm MORI and now running her own business, Wisdom Research & Marketing). Karen devised an innovative approach based on the 'Seven Up' British TV documentary series that tracked seven-year-old children every seven years through to adulthood. A 'typical' group of new joiners was followed at several key milestones during their first year. 'To gain depth of information and rationale behind their changing views, a series of individual depth interviews and focus groups were held on joining, mid-way through the intensive six-week training programme, on passing the training programme, after their first flight, one month after taking their first flight, at six months and at the end of the first year,' explains Karen.

A complementary questionnaire was also administered at key intervals, tracking key measures at an overall level throughout the journey (such as advocacy, job satisfaction, feeling informed, value and recognition, line manager relationship). In this way Karen could provide a 'mood barometer' to the airline using the aggregated scores from the group participants, and to track the performance of these key measures across the various milestones.

Valuable feedback from the first two milestones on the company's recruitment, induction and training processes indicated a number of practical suggestions for short term action. On joining, high levels of pride and excitement had been generated both from the company's strong external brand image and from the highly competitive recruitment process. Once recruited successfully, the candidates' morale was boosted by being made to feel that they were the 'chosen few'. Aspirations at this stage ran high and, despite the pressures of the intensive training programme, peaked further once the programme was completed, culminating in a 'passing out' ceremony.

However, Karen found that despite the build-up in morale over a period of several months, the whole group experienced a deflation in morale after experiencing their first flight as crew members. 'After being made to feel special, they now felt effectively "reduced" to the most junior of ranks and the least experienced employees in the hierarchy,' Karen noted, 'with a culture at that time accustomed to hierarchy and a reward system largely based on service length.'

Gradually the group began to feel cast adrift; the nature of their roles and demanding flight rosters meant they had little regular contact with a line manager (any contact being mainly with in-flight supervisors who varied by flight). No one felt as though their wellbeing, personal development or individual interests were being looked after. As time progressed, the excitement of a new job flying to new destinations was replaced by the 'lifestyle' of an airline crew member, the group's health began to suffer and niggling complaints started to emerge about rosters, systems and processes. They remained, however, willing to share experiences and their suggestions for improvements.

By the six-month stage, it became easy to predict which group members' commitment was being undermined by 'moments of truth', although their individual feedback remained confidential, in line with Market Research Society guidelines. By the six-month milestone, the group's collective commitment had started to waver significantly, with some members resigning to return to their former careers and others threatening to leave if matters did not improve. By the final end-of-year milestone, almost a third of the group had either left, resigned or were about to hand in resignations.

Due to the rolling nature of the programme, and the ongoing feedback process, a number of interventions were able to be made to the recruitment and induction processes relatively quickly. This showed an immediate benefit in retention levels among later groups of new joiners. In particular, the profile of those recruited was amended to reflect a greater emphasis on customer service experience.

In the longer term, this innovative approach to the issue by the airline helped to resolve the problems by creating better understanding of the issues. Steps were taken to manage the expectations of new recruits, the roll-out of a new management development programme focusing on coaching, mentoring and buddying activities and a review of performance management and reward systems. 'During the following year, whilst some of these initiatives were still being rolled out, a measurable reduction in attrition levels was experienced,' says Karen, 'which provided measurable ROI benefits to the business.'

- Leavers – at the other end of the equation are those who resign – in today's economic climate, the decision to leave is sometimes welcomed. What about the talented people the organization wants to keep? Don't just depend on the exit interview. In one project, the HR department became suspicious that the two reasons given – better prospects, more money – may not be accurate. Research among the leavers revealed relationship with the line manager was the prime cause, reinforcing the saying that 'people don't leave a company, they leave their manager.'
- There is a strong case for surveying the manager population separately. We all know the importance of the line manager – the annual survey results can look at their views as a separate group but there is a wealth of information that can be gained on specific issues close to their heart.
  - What are the main barriers stopping them doing their job better?
  - How could these be overcome?
  - What more support would be helpful from the communication and HR teams?
  - How seriously do they take their role in the communication chain?
  - In providing performance feedback?
  - Do they consider that their own managers provide sufficient information and encouragement to perform these tasks?

When is the most effective time to conduct the research? Senior management claiming 'now is not a good time' to 'let's wait until the change programme is over' are not good reasons to delay. 'Now' will never be a good moment: business change has become continual. However, there are times less propitious than others:

- Holiday times and festivals often mean that people's minds are elsewhere; indeed they may not even be at work during these periods.

- Try to time the results so they can be fed into any forward thinking such as the annual planning and budgeting cycles.

- If an announcement – about redundancies for example – is about to be publicized then uncertainty may colour views or opinions may be radically changed, making the results obsolete.

- Of course, an unexpected event may occur while the research is taking place. If this happens, turn this into an opportunity to look at views before and after to measure its impact.

In one case, a message announcing benefit reductions came out a few days following questionnaire circulation to employees. We were, therefore, able to look at responses before and after this announcement. Aspects like training, Intranet ratings etc, were unaffected. However, organizational advocacy and communication saw significant reductions, clearly showing the management team the effect of this action on certain areas.

Another timing issue is how often the research should be carried out or repeated. If there is a burning issue – prospect of a merger, for example – a frequent measure like a Pulse survey that comprises a few questions to take the temperature every few weeks during this period may be right. At the other end of the scale, a large international organization with slow action planning procedures may want to wait at least a year or more before revisiting the full research programme. The answer to this question is that it should be repeated when needed, whatever the timescale.

How should the research be conducted – by an external agency or internal resources? Until the advent of 'do-it-yourself' online tools to create surveys, external providers carried out much of the internal research, both design and delivery. There are still many good reasons for selecting professional help but in specific circumstances you may wish to consider using one of the tools now available to create your own survey. Bear in mind these points:

- For a large-scale research project, an external provider may well be the best choice. It could seem to be more costly up front, but take into account the hidden internal staff costs such as time taken/use of resources if carried out either by the IT department or others such as HR or communications.

- External professionals have a wide range of experience in carrying out such research and, apart from the technical expertise, are also well placed to interpret the results and provide perspective through comparisons with similar organizations, thus adding value.

- They are more likely to be seen as independent by employees, both from the viewpoint of producing trustworthy results and providing privacy for their individual responses. Senior management, too, sometimes find it easier to accept challenging findings from external experts in their field.

- If you decide to work with an external provider, do your homework to ensure that you are asking for proposals from agencies that can bring both research expertise and experience in communication/ employee research to the project. Some research companies have the former but not the latter, while other consultancies are knowledgeable about communication and HR issues but lack rigorous research techniques.

- Your brief for a proposal must be clear and concise. It should include your objectives, how you plan to use the results, whether such research has been carried out before, an outline of your organization (employee numbers, locations, etc), a desired timetable, feedback requirements (by function, location, etc and in what format), date proposal required and any other relevant information. An approximate budget is helpful in indicating the scale of the proposed project. This is sometimes avoided due to the suspicion the supplier will give a quote up to the maximum but it does help to know whether you have a Mini or Rolls Royce approach in mind. The brief should be clear but also allow opportunities for suggestions and ideas from those putting forward a proposal. Ensure you are contactable for any queries and don't do what some survey owners do – send out the brief just before going on holiday.

- Do give enough time for responses – if you want a considered, original proposal, you need to give the agencies sufficient notice to develop a response tailored to your specific needs within a reasonable time frame. If the proposal is for what is sometimes called a 'quickie' poll or just an initial ballpark response, two to three working days may be sufficient. Where a more considered approach is needed – perhaps including briefing meetings – 10 to 15 days would be a realistic time frame.

- Some organizations send out the brief to numerous agencies – this may not be as productive as they think. It is better to send the brief to three or four likely agencies with relevant experience and bring the final two in for a personal meeting before making the decision. Alternatively, you may wish to meet up with several agencies before asking a couple for a full proposal. More is not necessarily better: remember that you will have to take the time to field their queries and review their submissions.

- For smaller scale and specific studies (for instance a recent event or announcement), you may wish to consider carrying this out internally. In that case, you could use an external web provider who will set up your questionnaire and host this externally, saving internal resources and giving respondents confidence about the independence of the provider.

- Alternatively you may wish to use one of the online tools to create your own survey quickly and easily. No software needs to be installed and these enable you to make a professional-looking questionnaire, send a link to employees for completion and then review the results and even create your own charts. Leading survey tools are SurveyMonkey and Zoomerang but there are many others available. The downside: such tools may be easy to set up and use, thus creating a situation where poorly designed questionnaires appear. It is also a recipe for various departments to carry out surveys on a whole range of issues without any kind of central control or standards. There needs to be some overall responsibility to stop questionnaires dropping into people's in-boxes too frequently.

- If you are carrying out your own research, you may get advice from an internal research department if one exists in your organization, while some external web providers will take the data and format this for you if needed. For those carrying out their own research internally, you will need to be aware of how best to achieve an effective, efficient research programme. This book provides practical, constructive advice and information to help you achieve robust and reliable data for decision making.

There are two other frequent questions: how much and how long will it take? Again, the answers depend on a number of factors. With today's speedy technology advances, it is possible to get feedback within a day or so of questionnaire completion. So for a fast-turnaround short survey, time could be quick. However, taking into account the initial considered planning through to the development of feedback and action planning, the entire process from inception to completion will have a longer time span. For a widespread international conglomerate, the whole project might take up to five months, while an average research project might be around two or three months in its entirety. The same broad parameters apply to budgets. An instant phone survey carried out internally will only cost your/team time and that of the people you interview. The extensive worldwide employee survey covering thousands with translations and reporting back to each department will cost considerably more. The main question is whether the investment is worthwhile. One manager explained that he had calculated that the research cost was two per cent of his total budget and, as the results enabled him to direct budget into the most productive channels, this investment proved its value. Do the maths yourself to assess the worth to your business.

Research from your desk

Before starting on your research journey, arm yourself with as much information as you can gain 'from your desk'. There is a wealth of information already within your organization – turn detective to find these metrics, which could include:

- Profile of your people – age, gender, average service length.
- Business statistics such as successful initiatives launched, new products.
- Public sector/not-for profit metrics such as efficiency, service levels.

- Customer service levels, complaints, letters of praise.
- Employee statistics such as turnover, absenteeism, retention, job offers refused, exit interviews, suggestions scheme participation.
- Level of grievances/disciplinary procedures.
- Any issues raised through briefing meetings, Town Hall meetings, etc.
- 'Chat' on the Intranet – and any external sites where employees may make their feelings known.
- Existing research from other functions such as marketing and brand image about your organization's image, reputation drivers and media analysis.

This is just a starter list – look around, you will find others. These will help to both plan any internal research and also understand and interpret the results with authority. There are also many reports and external surveys carried out by survey agencies and others that give useful information – some are listed in the Appendix.

Remember

- Consult, but ensure you are not swamped with requests for irrelevant questions.
- Balance carefully the options of professional help – and the advantages that will bring – against conducting your own research internally.
- Don't forget that you can learn much from existing data and research into your organization's image externally.
- Think about special groups of staff such as new recruits; specific information would be useful rather than automatically surveying everybody in the organization.
- Spend sufficient time and thought defining the aims of the measurement and desired outcomes such as behaviour change. Time spent in planning and preparation is never wasted.

Involving and communicating with employees

02

Make the research process an integral part of your organization by providing information about the project and listening to colleague views.

You have fallen at the first hurdle if the first employees know about your research programme is when the questionnaire pops up on their screen or drops on to their desk. Of course, if this is a small-scale project involving only a small proportion of employees, only those participating may need to be informed.

For organization-wide studies, it is essential to communicate with employees and create an environment where they will feel involved in the process. The first step is to start a conversation at senior levels, as described earlier, to ensure full commitment and interest from the top.

- Find ways to link business or public value metrics and the planned research programme and ask senior management to suggest others. What behaviour changes are they expecting from their people as a result of their strategy and plans – and what involvement and contribution do they expect that might improve these metrics?

- Ask them to define what information about employees the leadership needs to know to move the business forward that could be included in regular senior management feedback.

- Share some of the extensive findings that show links between business productivity/financial success/performance/efficiency and so-called softer aspects like communication and human resource issues to 'prove the case' for the research (see Chapter 11).

- Plan to send regular updates to senior managers so that they are informed about project progress and it remains front of mind.

- The next group to persuade will be managers – both those with team responsibility and also managers of specific functions. Research among their people can sometimes be viewed as a threat, detracting from their support and interest. You will need to address this.

- Allay the possible concerns about the results being a stick to beat them with by explaining upfront that this will be useful management information to help them in their role, and give them some examples of the format in which their results will be provided and how action planning can be approached.

- Share that valuable information about the linkages between communication, engagement and performance so they understand this is not a dry as dust exercise but will have a real benefit to the business.

- Find case studies of successful research projects, preferably from organizations in the same market, to show what can be achieved.

- Ask them for any metrics or data from their area capable of being measured against the research outcomes to show any linkages that could help the business.

- Explain that this will be useful to help them manage and engage their team in the business. Involve them by finding out which format methods they find most informative and easy to use – and then how action planning can be approached.

- Persuade managers to talk about the survey and mention this at team meetings or other appropriate points so that it becomes an accepted part of business planning.

- As suggested earlier, consultation with colleagues in other functions will help develop a measurement approach and content that delivers to business needs.

- The fourth group for involvement and communication will be the wider workforce. Some may be involved in helping to develop the questionnaire (see Chapter 6). Communication with employees generally is essential both to promote the response rate and also to capture their interest for the action planning stage (see Chapter 7).

- At an early stage, manage expectations: this will not be a free-for-all of impossible aspirations but a process both of listening to employees and understanding more about the business.

- Publish an outline plan with an estimated date for feedback to employees and the form this will take (eg will each team have its own results?).

- Create a website to inform about the progress of the project and give background information about the value of internal research, with a few brief case studies of practical examples of action which have led to improvements.

A communication campaign of emails and posters could be helpful here depending on the organizational profile. In a retail organization with a young workforce, perhaps many part-timers, a fun approach with eye-catching branding and ways of presenting the results can capture attention. To achieve this in one health organization, the results were divided into 'doing well', 'feeling poorly' and 'needs urgent treatment'.

CASE STUDY 3 State of Georgia Government, USA: major role for employees in research programme

'Our most important strategy was to involve employees in identifying and creating the workplace they desire, in collaboration with leadership,' said Justine Holcomb who specializes in employee-focused communications with the State of Georgia, USA, describing their role in providing customer-service excellence. 'Our employee teams were tasked with talking to their peers to learn what works well and what needs improvement. They used the survey results to focus their conversations on major pain points.

Improvement of service quality, efficiency and productivity in Georgia government by engaging state employees in shaping a customer-focused culture had been a focus since 2006, when Justine helped lead a first-of-its-kind campaign promoting customer-service excellence in government, with communications programmes and materials targeting more than 100,000 state and university employees. Three years later she also helped launch a special programme to improve employee satisfaction among Georgia government workers. For both campaigns, employee involvement and empowerment were essential strategies.

Justine's team saw direct links between a satisfied, engaged workforce and better customer service so there were crucial reasons for adopting this approach. 'Our work was especially important in a tough economic climate; tax revenues and state budgets were decreasing while more citizens needed public services,' said Justine. 'We needed to maximize existing resources to deliver better value to the community.'

Retaining a high-performing, engaged workforce would be key to delivering quality service. Georgia leaders saw an opportunity to help state agencies increase employee satisfaction as a complement to their customer-service focus. In 2009, Justine's team brought a pilot group of eight state agencies of varying sizes and services together, representing about 24,000 employees, to test and prove this concept.

Each agency designated a 'champion', typically a senior human-resources or communications professional, to lead improvement efforts internally. The group's overall goal was to develop and prove a model for improving employee job satisfaction in state government. Their primary objective was to increase overall employee-satisfaction survey scores by two points in one year. The model consisted of key approaches that could be tailored to fit the needs and culture of each organization:

- conduct annual employee surveys;

- enlist employee-led teams to conduct peer interviews;

- empower employees to generate ideas and actions for improvement;

- foster collaborative relationships and mutual accountability with employees and management.

Justine pointed out that the group used the survey results to focus their conversations on major pain points. The next important stage was that management empowered them to report problems and recommend solutions.'

The teams then went a step further. 'Often, employee feedback is presented to management, and employees wait for management to fix things,' noted Justine. 'We expected our employees to take the lead in the implementation phase as well, leveraging individual interests, skills and passions to ensure sustainability.'

The surveys and interviews guided specific strategies and tactics within each agency. Within her own organization, Justine saw that a few simple, yet focused efforts led by employees reaped the greatest gains in satisfaction.

One effort focused on promoting training opportunities. 'When we interviewed our colleagues, we found that many perceived an overall lack of support for professional development, believing that there was no budget, no time and little encouragement from management,' said Justine. 'Our team suspected this was a communication issue and asked management to clarify their stance. Management agreed to commit a small budget and specified number of hours per year for training, and to include training in employee development plans. We put these commitments in writing and shared them with all staff. We also researched existing training programs within state government, finding a variety of options from computer-based modules to toastmasters. We began promoting these on a monthly basis in staff meetings.'

Employees also voiced a common frustration that management would make changes late in the process of projects, leading to confusion and distrust. 'Our colleagues wanted more structured dialogue, from meetings to regular reports, with opportunities for questions and feedback,' said Justine. 'We encouraged individual leaders to have more one-on-one dialogue with their staff members, while we took charge of other ways to facilitate better communication within the organization.' For example, Justine's team restructured weekly staff meetings to run more efficiently and add greater value for employees. They collected staff and manager input to develop tips for 'communicating for clarity' and had everyone role-play the tips in a staff meeting.

Finally, team members developed a simple recognition programme driven by peer nominations and voting. Employees indicated that they didn't expect much in terms of financial rewards, but they really wanted some appreciation for their efforts. Once a quarter, employees were invited to nominate peers for excellence in service and then vote for the best nominees. Everyone recognized the winners in a simple, fun ceremony.

The approach and activities paid off. In the second annual survey, the overall improvement among all agencies was four percentage points – double the established objective. Seven of the eight agencies saw increased satisfaction, with Justine's own organization reaping the largest gains:

- overall workplace satisfaction in her agency improved by 16 points, or 25 per cent;

- the rating for 'management expectations are clear' jumped 21 points;

- the rating for 'training opportunities are available' jumped 40 points;

- the rating for 'opportunities for special recognition' jumped 54 points.

'Our work on a few key areas elevated satisfaction in a majority of areas, like a rising tide lifting all boats,' observed Justine. 'The very act of involving employees was perhaps more influential than any particular activities.'

A degree of involvement will be provided by discussions to help develop the questionnaire (see Chapter 4). But why not give the opportunity to all to suggest 'top topics' they would like to see covered via emails, team meetings or suggestion boxes? Clearly this would need to be carefully managed to avoid being buried under a pile of information and the expectation that all ideas will be included. It would, however, involve all in the process and give them the opportunity to contribute from the outset.

Consider the formation of a survey project group drawn from different parts of the organization, functions and levels. This has proved very successful in some places. It need not be time-consuming for those taking part, but regular meetings help gain feedback and create survey supporters who can help with driving up response rates as well as the future action planning. Clear guidelines will be needed so that the group keeps to its remit and does not, for example, see this as a free-for-all to add in questions.

As an extension of this idea, why not have a team of survey 'champions'? There are usually enthusiastic people around an organization who welcome an opportunity to do something different and interesting; to motivate and involve them, an explanation of the how and why of the research will get them on board. These are people – especially in larger organizations – who can act as active enthusiasts to convince colleagues to participate and act as your eyes and ears for what is happening at grass-roots level. Publicize their role so others know that their co-workers are part of the team. It can also be helpful if people are concerned about anonymity. In one case this was dispelled by having a small group of 'survey champions' visit the data-processing firm where the questionnaires were analysed and seeing for themselves the process and hearing at first hand the commitment not to identify individual responses.

As you talk to colleagues, you may find that they are thinking of carrying out research for their own function. Emphasis on gaining feedback – especially for departmental customer satisfaction – combined with easy access to online survey tools can be a toxic mix of a free-for-all survey mania. To keep this in check – without losing their enthusiasm – why not have a regular survey where others needing feedback can join in by submitting questions that can be included. This would be on similar lines to the omnibus approach of research agencies where, to save time and costs, several research requirements with specific questions are combined into one overall survey among the general public or specific audiences. In this way, you can control the quality and frequency while supplying the requisite feedback. As some firms have rules about all staff emails only when essential, the same could apply to feedback surveys – your colleagues will be less likely to do their own thing if this facility is available to them to gain the information required.

Remember

- Make a convincing case for the research and share the extensive range of case studies that show the links with business.
- Communicate a clear timeline and aims for the research.
- Organize a regular survey that other functions can 'buy-into' when they need feedback on their services/initiatives.
- Talk to and involve colleagues at all levels throughout your organization – their role in developing the research is key to having a relevant process that leads to commitment to action planning.

Data or discussion?

03

Next we look at the various research methods, both quantitative and qualitative – these are not mutually exclusive but you need to understand what each offers to decide which is right for your project.

Your decision on whether to choose a questionnaire-based quantitative approach or qualitative focus group discussions – or a combination of both – will depend on what you want from the research. Quantitative is based on analysis of numerical data (such as '60 per cent think communication should be faster') while qualitative probes feelings, opinions and behaviours (such as 'there is a strong sense that communication should be faster, particularly in times of change').

The hard data from quantitative research can often be more convincing to management. It is difficult to argue with firm numbers, whereas outputs from focus groups are sometimes disregarded as the opinions of a minority or just 'moan sessions'. Other advantages of this approach are:

- Provision of firm facts and statistically reliable figures on which to base decisions and direct initiatives and programmes.

- The ability to compare results over time to measure progress.

- Analysis by location, job role, department provides information to drill down into specific employee groups while preserving individual anonymity.

- Comparisons with other organizations where similar questions have been used.

- Statistical techniques can be used for analysis to add value to the results.

- All employees can be included and have the opportunity to express their views. This sends an important message about how much the organization values listening to individual employees, assuming, of course, that action is taken on their views.

- If it becomes clear that a quantitative approach is what is required, the next decision is what questionnaire collection system will be best.

There is a toolkit of various methods available to you and these need to be reviewed and considered carefully before proceeding.

Web surveys

With the facility offered via the web, online surveys are most commonly used nowadays. Here the questionnaire is set up online and a link sent to employees invited to take part. By clicking on the link, people access the questionnaire and go through page by page clicking on each of their responses. Often a bar at the top shows how far participants have got through the questionnaire. The advantages of this approach are:

- Speed – responses are registered instantly.
- Cost – the main expense is in putting the questionnaire online, the number of respondents answering makes little difference to the overall cost as they are inputting the data directly so it gives better value for large-scale surveys.
- Accuracy – avoids possible data-processing mistakes. It also means that if people click on more than one option when a single answer is wanted, this can be flagged up immediately with the instruction to only select one response.
- Ability to ask specific questions following on from certain responses, eg if there is a negative response, a further question can ask: 'Why do you say that?'
- Easy to send reminders of the closing date to encourage participation.
- Online is more popular with young people accustomed to electronic communication via the web with Facebook, Twitter, etc.
- Suitable for international surveys as this speeds the process, avoiding postal complications and delays.

However, there are some disadvantages:

- Could disenfranchise those who do not have web access at work or are unused to using a computer.
- Can cause more concern about anonymity – if government websites can be hacked, some may be concerned that online surveys might be accessed internally, too, and their responses tracked to them as individuals.

Paper-based postal or group self-completion surveys

Where many employees are working on the shop floor in manufacturing/ retail environments or similar with no facility for online access, printed paper questionnaires may be more appropriate. Here you will need to consider the following:

- Questionnaires are printed and distributed with reply-paid envelopes for return. For convenience and to save costs, one double-sided sheet can contain both the questions and return address to be folded and sealed to post.

- Try to address questionnaires to individuals to ensure receipt and emphasize the value of their individual contribution. Just sending out a pile of forms for people to pick up at some central point is not conducive to persuading them to take part. Some organizations provide a central point internally for returns, in which case you must ensure that these are secure from tampering before going for processing.

When I was communication manager for an international company, employees were asked to return questionnaires in the internal postbox, which sat on the local manager's desk. One person phoned me: 'How can you guarantee that my manager does not open the envelope and read my answers?' she asked. I could not. They may be the exception rather than the rule, but managers have been known to ask their team not to seal their envelopes before returning them via him or her personally. One wonders why.

- Postal surveys, especially in organizations where people are not office-based, can generate lower response rates as these employees may be less accustomed to filling in forms than desk-based colleagues. To ensure a better level of return, another option is to arrange group sessions for questionnaire completion. Groups of employees are invited to a room with a facilitator where they complete the questionnaire before it is collected. This has a further advantage in cases where workers may not be fully comfortable with English or are semi-literate – here the facilitator can read out the questions and deal with queries.

- Care needs to be taken so that people are not intimidated, so it is best if groups can be at similar job levels to ensure they feel comfortable with each other.

- Where the survey is carried out by an external research agency, professional facilitators will be available to carry out this task. This reassures those taking part about their independence. Usually up to about 25 to 35 people can be accommodated in this way in one-hour sessions. In one large car manufacturing plant, when the workers finished their shift they came to the large hall where the instructions were read out before completing the questionnaire. About 200 people a time participated – with several agency facilitators to hand out/collect forms and respond to queries. It certainly took some organization – but the firm was rewarded with a response rate of 80 per cent plus, which it would never have achieved otherwise.

- It is possible to use internal people as facilitators. However, this needs to be carefully handled. If colleagues at a similar level to those attending facilitate, this provides some reassurance. Line managers or the human resource or communication departments might raise suspicion about confidentiality. Such a team will need to be fully briefed to carry out their task objectively, to ensure, for example, that they do not make any comments or suggestions that might influence answers.

- Although online facilities may not be easily accessible at work, many people now have computers at home – they could be given a link so if they prefer to complete a questionnaire in this way out of working hours, they can do so.

Face-to-face interviews

Interviews carried out in person, face-to-face, are usually associated with external research studies, but there is no reason why this method could not be used internally, provided anonymity is assured for those being interviewed.

- You need to consider logistical problems, such as where and when to speak to employees, as this type of approach will only be suitable for short, snappy interviews. However, where a low response rate is expected, this could be an option to ensure you reach your target audience.

- If you decide to use an external agency, professional interviewers are likely to collect responses using CAPI (Computer Assisted Personal Interviews). Here the interviewer keys the responses directly into a purpose-built computer program using a small hand-held device or laptop. In practical terms, due to cost/time implications, the numbers actually interviewed might be relatively low but results are immediate so this is a useful option in the research toolkit.

- Making use of an internal team to facilitate this process is possible.

In my internal communication manager days, I had a team of about 10 people worldwide – my Contact Team – tasked with carrying out an occasional quick survey on my behalf. I could email out a few questions, such as reaction to the new format journal or changes to the training programme, asking them to interview about 10 people and within a day I had 100-plus responses. This could not be described as strict 'measurement' but did give me fast feedback on current topics. A word of warning: the team does need thorough briefing to ensure they do not 'lead' those they approach or just go to the same friends each time. Such a briefing note might look like this.

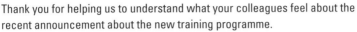

Briefing note for the Contact Team

Thank you for helping us to understand what your colleagues feel about the recent announcement about the new training programme.

We would like you to ask the questions below of 10 people in your area. This is not 'scientific' research but will give us a good idea of reactions.

When selecting those to interview please do not just go to friends or those you know well. To give a representative view they should be a mix of male/female with both long and short service in different roles in your part of the business.

Ask the questions in a direct way and, so they will not be influenced, do not discuss the topic beforehand or comment on their answers.

Please do this today if at all possible and send the answers back with a total for each question. Before you start, explain that you have a few questions and this will only take a minute or two of their time.

1 Have you heard anything about the training programme recently?

Yes   No   Don't know

(If yes, continue)

2 Do you know that a new training programme has been introduced?

Yes   No   Don't know

(if yes continue)

3 How helpful for your own development do you think this programme will be?

Very   Quite   Not very   Not at all   Don't know

4 Why do you say that?

Telephone

Another option is to telephone a sample of employees based either on a set questionnaire or an open interview.

- If this is a large-scale study, you will want to consider using an external telephone research company. They are likely to be using Computer Assisted Telephone Interviews, along similar lines to CAPI. The interviewer will phone the person to be interviewed and input the responses directly into the questionnaire that has been set up on their system. This tends to be an expensive option so you need to consider whether the information gathered will be sufficiently valuable.

- Telephone interviews can also be used to gain spontaneous feedback through interviews – especially appropriate for senior managers who may be short of time or for those working from home or overseas where face-to-face interviews may be expensive or otherwise logistically impractical.

- Whatever your approach, it is essential that the interviewees are briefed in advance lest they refuse to speak to an unknown person on the phone. You will also have to bear in mind that answers may be overheard in an open-plan office, which may inhibit the interview. In this case, responses could be assigned numbers to call out (eg one equals strongly agree) or an appropriate time and place agreed so that they can have some privacy for their answers. Perhaps a room can be arranged so that the conversation is not overheard by others.

- Some customer telephone surveys use automated systems whereby responses are keyed in or spoken to the phone – up to now these have not been used much for employee research but could well be an option in the future for short, direct research.

Combining methodologies

Market research purists may dislike mixing quantitative methodologies – it could be that the process chosen influences responses in some way, thus producing skewed results among the different audiences. However, in the context of employee research and in practical terms, a combination of online, print and telephone may be a pragmatic solution. Indeed, use of a variety of research approaches is sometimes encouraged to provide a more comprehensive, rounded picture.

- In some organizations certain members of staff may have easy online access, while others do not. In which case it is sensible to mix print and online approaches – the returns can be combined to give an overall result.

- A mix of quantitative mixed with qualitative is particularly useful to provide a more complete picture – hard data plus insights into the reasons behind attitudes works very well to give a better overall sense of people's attitudes and feelings.

However, these approaches are not mutually exclusive. Qualitative has quite different functions. It can be used pre or post the questionnaire phase to:

- Help develop the questionnaire, in which case the approach will be open to gain spontaneous views from people, based on topics envisaged for that questionnaire with the opportunity to raise other hot issues that need to be included. Listening to the phrases and terms that employees typically use means that the questionnaire can be written in their language.

- Explore or explain puzzling or ambiguous findings from the quantitative stage – this means that the discussion will be focused on the findings from the questionnaire-based survey.
- Research a specific topic as a separate, stand-alone exercise. This will be perhaps an initial 'toe in the water' or to gain feedback without a major exercise involving the whole organization.

A range of approaches – usually face-to-face, occasionally telephone and with the advent of online techniques, via the web – are used for qualitative research (covered more fully in the next chapter).

With fast-changing technology bringing new opportunities to the capture of information for measurement, it is vital to keep up-to-date with any fresh methodologies that may be developed, such as online communities which are frequently used for research among customers and other groups. So far, these online communities have been used mainly externally but there is no reason why they should not be extended for internal feedback.

Online communities

Andy Buckley, head of research at Join the Dots, believes such platforms have much to offer. He envisages an employee community using the same type of platform as for customer research, which all employees would be invited to join. This would be 'always on' for employees who could share knowledge and ideas while break-out discussions could also take place on the same platform. 'This would allow employers to more effectively tap into the thoughts and feelings of employees,' believes Andy, 'to help create, manage and nurture a more engaged workforce.'

Another organization with a strong belief in the potential of online communities is the research agency, Opinion Leader. Their in-house platform CaucusWorld provides online discussion groups, particularly useful for geographically diverse people. It can also run instant feedback surveys with the ability to stream multimedia straight to participants' desktops.

At present these methods are mainly used for external research among customers or other discrete groups and seldom seem to be used internally. However, they do have great potential to be added to the feedback mix providing another opportunity for listening to views. Such platforms cannot completely replace more traditional research methods. Ray Poynter of the Future Place, the thought leader consultancy, suggests that online communities are best for collaborative innovation and product/process improvement rather than measurement per se. 'One major consideration,' he says, 'is anonymity. Here there is a greater risk that even if people use names and images that do not reveal their identity, they may say something that gives them away.'

His point that social media is *best used for collaborative networks* is illustrated by such examples as the Fix It people at Best Buy in North America where the self-named 'geek squad' have a great online network where they regularly share ideas and suggestions online.

Remember

- Consider very carefully what outcomes/feedback you need before choosing a quantitative or qualitative approach.
- Select which quantitative method is best for your organization.
- Ensure that the process is organized efficiently – mistakes undermine the authority of the research.
- Keep an open mind about what fresh methods may emerge, especially those offered by social media.

Conversation 2
Don't underestimate the impact of social media: **Marc Wright**, chairman, simply-communicate

The world of communication has been transformed by the continuing growth of social media. The following figures will have increased even as you read these pages: 110 million blogs, 100 million videos a day watched on YouTube and enough population on Facebook to constitute a major world power.

What impact will this have on the measurement and evaluation of internal communication? There are three main influences to consider according to social media expert Marc Wright, founder of simply-communicate – the knowledge site for internal communication professionals. Marc takes a keen interest in the application of social media and Web 2.0 inside large organizations.

'Opportunities through these new social business media have extended ownership of communication to employees as well as the traditional internal channels previously owned by the management,' explains Marc. 'This means that people can find out much more information about their organization – negative as well as positive – as they surf the net. So I would advise organizations to extend their measurement of internal channels to include these external sources to get a realistic picture of communication sources.'

'Employees who are not given a forum to express themselves will soon find one in the external blogosphere' says Marc, giving two examples to illustrate this second point. 'www.browncafe.com is an unofficial site set up by UPS staff to discuss every issue under the sun about working for the delivery company. Set up in 1999, the home page clearly states "not sponsored or endorsed by UPS" while it describes itself as a "unique site designed for mainly UPS employees to exchange information, learn new techniques about their job, methods in dealing with management or job stresses, or just an area to kick back and sound off". Now UPS is trying to fight back by making their own intranet more appealing and transparent,' explains Marc, 'but it appears that the horse has bolted. The pirate site has grabbed the radio station and is doing a very good job at meeting the needs of this online population.'

Where employees themselves are setting up their own forums to share feedback with each other the internal upward communication channels – including internal surveys – may not be working as effectively as they might. 'These forums give people the chance to discuss issues and concerns,' says Marc, 'and it's anonymous – they can give a "handle" rather than their name so these employee-owned sites are often more open, and thus more popular, than internal feedback.'

An exception is the insurance group Aviva, which has made their staff forums a success on Aviva World by espousing a liberal attitude to what threads they publish. 'They also have a personal as well as a business section,' Marc explains. 'The argument goes that if you get people on to a social forum dealing with non-work issues, it gets them used to the channel and they are more ready to take their work-based issues online.'

According to Marc, measurement of such employee feedback provides useful insight. Comments can be categorized – as in external media evaluation – into tone of voice: positive, neutral and negative. This can be tracked over time, which could also measure the impact of any internal messages.

Looking ahead, Marc foresees an exciting opportunity to 'mine the internal data'. Programmes exist to carry this out externally so messages and offers can be focused on those who have shown an interest through their web usage. 'So far this has not taken off internally,' he explains, 'but when it does, this will bring a new perspective to measurement.' He gives as an example: employees who might access the Health and Safety website where visits can be measured for specific subjects and information communicated back to those visitors where interest is greatest.

'This data mining will also pick up topics mentioned most frequently among specific audiences to give fast measurement to hot topics and emerging issues', says Marc. 'For instance, at BT they use the searches that staff use on the internal Intranet to assess what colleagues are really interested in. So if there is a spike in interest in, say, appraisals, then this might mean that the online advice on this subject might need to be reviewed and refreshed. Another key advantage of this kind of data is to change the way information is described on a company's Intranet. If you are getting hundreds of searches on "booking a holiday" you might want to stop calling that form "Annual Leave requisition".'

Another powerful use of social media for internal measurement is what is loosely called 'social search'. As staff fill in their mySite profiles (or whatever social media system is in play) they are laying down information about their skills, likes, areas of interest and capabilities. IBM is one of a rising number of social business-savvy operations that are tagging the activities of colleagues to make them more easily found by others with a specific need. The conferences they have attended, papers they write, projects they are involved with – all this data can be used to identify the knowledge resources and networks that drive collaboration and productivity.

From a measurement perspective there is the opportunity to track where and how messages flow through an organization. Called Social Network Analysis this is a potentially significant tool that can measure and identify the 'connectors' who can help messages go viral and the 'bottlenecks' who are stifling communication in a function or area of a business. The power of these tools still lies in the future, but there is much excitement around the promise of real-time measurement of employee behaviour that these new techniques allow. When who you are reading, what you are posting, how you rate documents and processes and how you are spending your time can all be monitored in real time it will be possible to see how employees are reacting to different stimuli and ways of working. Put in feedback loops and then we can make continuous improvement in our service operations in the same way that manufacturing processes have been revolutionized through kaizen.

Another advantage of such real-time measurement is that it can be more objective as it reflects workforce opinion and actions as they happen – rather than what employees choose to tell in a more formal survey. This empirical data is often more convincing for senior management, although the sheer weight of information can be unwieldy and expensive to analyse.

Marc adds:

> We have worked with a number of companies to use the wisdom of crowds to make such data more manageable. So for instance we have asked staff about their concerns during a major merger of two retail banks. This generated thousands of comments, but by combining themes and then getting staff themselves to vote on what are the key issues we have been able to establish what were the real pain points and advise the HR experts accordingly as they conducted negotiations with the unions.

'It is not research *per se*,' says Marc, 'but surely the more methods we have to collect feedback the better! Anybody rejecting the new is a King (or Queen) Canute. That is my view anyway!'

Qualitative techniques and methods

04

An introduction to discussion and interview approaches and methods to set up, manage, facilitate and interpret feedback.

'Just talking' to people can seem an easy option to gain information. However, getting groups of employees together for discussions can have a downside. Indeed, management sometimes dismiss such discussions as moan sessions and, unless carefully managed, this is what can happen. Inviting employees to focus group sessions to talk things through may only provide a medium for a list of complaints and grumbles, leading nowhere.

However, conducted effectively, qualitative research has the potential to gain an in-depth understanding of attributes, opinions and behaviours and the reasons behind them. It is an opportunity to dig below the surface and challenge vague comments to gain specific examples. The approach can be adapted for different audiences and build on comments and suggestions as the project progresses.

To avoid the negative approach that management fear, good facilitation is essential. The facilitator moderates a focus group that normally comprises a discussion among a group of individuals who share interests, circumstances or background, in this case employees working for the same organization. Who should act as facilitator? Qualitative professionals with specialist expertise have extensive training and experience, often using specific techniques. These are expert moderators who also analyse the feedback, interpret the results and develop recommendations.

If for reasons of cost or timing it is decided to carry out qualitative work internally, it is best carried out by perceived independent people rather than, for example, line managers. Some organizations train a small team or use internal communicators. This approach will only be successful if a number of fundamental principles are kept in mind. You need to think about:

- selecting the participants;
- organizing a suitable location;
- developing a topic guide;
- facilitating the group or the interview;
- transcripts – which may be required – so discussions can be taped (although this may be disturbing for employees concerned about their personal anonymity);
- interpreting and presenting the feedback.

CASE STUDY 4 Tetra Pak: how talking about core values showed a way ahead

For several decades an integral part of the Tetra Pak culture had been its core values. As an international organization with head offices in Sweden and Switzerland, Tetra Pak provides processing and packaging for food, employing 22,000-plus people around the world in over 170 countries. With such a diverse workforce and the many global changes since the values were first defined, the question arose about how much these core values are known, understood and lived throughout the organization.

'We set out to find how our core values support our strategy, vision and brand – and how they were being lived,' explains Nancy Helledie, Vice President of Communication Excellence, who managed the project to find the answer. There had been many internal discussions about the core values in the past few years. 'It was important not to repeat what had already been discovered,' she says. 'Previous discussions revealed potential issues with the core values and shifts in the company culture, but these were not yet clearly defined so more concrete information was needed to inform our decision making around the Core Values – whether the core values were still relevant today and should there be any changes to better support our business.'

The first step made best use of the material already gathered to combine this into one overview document which summarized this feedback and also revealed any extra insight that was needed. A qualitative approach of focus groups and in-depth interviews was chosen as the most constructive way forward. 'To move beyond the information already gathered,' explains Nancy, 'we needed guidance on the behaviours associated with each of the core values which could only come from in-depth conversations.'

Working with a team from the simply-communicate consultancy, Nancy faced the challenge of deciding where and how these conversations should be arranged. With such a widespread organization, it was impractical to include every location. 'But we wanted to ensure that the views of our people working in different countries were reflected as well as our home base in Sweden,' she says. The solution was to set up focus groups in the emerging markets of China, Pakistan and Brazil as well as the longer established locations in Italy and Sweden plus in-depth telephone interviews with senior management. Country qualitative specialists who could conduct the discussions in the local language were identified in the first three countries and fully briefed so that feedback would be consistent.

Next, the specific questions were developed in line with aims of the research. First, to ascertain the extent to which the values formed part of working life, employees were asked how they would describe Tetra Pak to see whether they mentioned aspects of the five core values. Next they were given 15 to 20 options of values that they might identify with Tetra Pak, to see if they could select those that are real values.

Moving into specifics, each value was taken in turn to see if these represented Tetra Pak in the eyes of its people. Then they were asked what behaviours and examples they see demonstrated by their colleagues – both positive and negative – for each value.

Turning to the future, they were asked what values they feel are needed to take the company forward that are not present in the current five and whether any of the current core values are no longer relevant to today's business context.

The feedback from these discussions plus the senior manager in-depth interviews revealed strong support for the core values and recognition of their significant value to Tetra Pak. However, it was also evident that clearer understanding was needed across the company since the values were interpreted differently in different countries – depending on the country company culture. This was no surprise since Tetra Pak has been growing quickly over many years as a very decentralized and entrepreneurial company.

'This was an important piece of work,' said Nancy, 'which we used to inform the decision-making on the core values internally in Tetra Pak. Not only did a qualitative approach give deeper insight into current views but it also helped to focus relevant action for the future. Some minor updates were made to the Tetra Pak core values in 2009 and they were reinvigorated as part of a company-wide internal employee engagement programme and continue to be critical to the company's success.'

How many groups/interviews are needed?

Remember here that we are looking for quality rather than quantity. We are seeking insight and understanding rather than counting numbers of participants. Clearly, one or two groups may not provide the information – or confidence – you will need, but dozens of groups may not give much more additional, valuable information.

There is no formula to decide on the number of groups or interviews. Although a statistically reliable representative sample is not the purpose here, you will need to consider the profile of the workforce and where they are based. So typically you will want at least one or two groups per level/grade, with function also represented. With a geographically spread organization, you should also consider location/country – not all have to be covered, but you will need to have some sense that the feedback covers different viewpoints.

There may also be political aspects to take into account. To give an example, one organization insisted that a specific country was included as 'they always felt left out and will not believe the results unless they are represented'. Thus some additional groups were added, not for additional information but to gain acceptance for the results.

Three or four groups in a small organization may well be sufficient, but in a widespread, large organization, you may not need more than about 12 or so groups.

Another consideration is time away from work. An average time for a focus group is around an hour and a half – this may be shorter if the focus is one topic or longer if a number of issues, exercises or projective techniques (see below) are used.

Once you have selected your locations – perhaps the head office and three others – you will need to consider selecting those who will participate.

Selecting the participants

An easy option may seem just to ask people to volunteer to participate. There may be a few occasions when this is appropriate but there is a downside to self-selection. It could bring an attitudinal bias – people who have a particular viewpoint they want to put forward, either positive or negative. Moreover, their profile may not reflect the workforce and may be skewed towards a particular grade, level or function. A rigorous scientific approach to sampling is not needed as it is for a quantitative survey. However, reasonably typical representation is required to gain a more complete picture of employee opinions and attitudes.

- To gain a more typical profile, names can be drawn at random across the location to receive an invitation to take part. The downside here is that it may produce a quiet group with little to say or contribute.

- What you want, will be people willing to speak out and express their opinions. So it can be best to ask the human resources department or local managers to help by asking them to suggest suitable people to participate. This may seem risky in case they select those with positive views – but in practice I have not found this to be an issue. However, do give them an outline of those to invite in terms of age, gender, function, level, etc so the group at least approximately represents the profile of the workforce. This need not be a completely representative sample, but does provide a rough outline to suggest potential participants. Concern has been expressed that this approach allows those selecting employees just to invite 'yes' people so it is also worthwhile suggesting that a few people known to be outspoken are included. So far I have never found managers subvert the exercise by only choosing very positive people.

- When it comes to numbers in the group, more is not better. The optimum number is six to eight. Any number over 10 makes it difficult to keep eye contact and ensure that all have a chance to speak.

- As some will be unable to attend, invitations need to be sent out with plenty of time to allow for responses and additional invitations where refusals are returned.

Those responses are essential. At one local authority, as the facilitator, I will never forget waiting in vain for anybody to turn up to the first group and only one person to the second. The fact that this single employee had only come along as he was in a lonely job working in a park and wanted to make contact with other colleagues was particularly ironic. Later it transpired that the organizer did not want to 'pester' those invited by asking them to respond with an acceptance/refusal. So it is essential to follow up – even with a phone call/email on the day as a reminder.

At the other end of the scale, an experience at another local authority taught me the value of being very firm with the ground rules. We had asked for two groups with about seven in each and suggested inviting 10 to allow for dropouts. Our contact thought she would be helpful and doubled the number, asking the regional contact for 20. That person also thought they would be helpful and again doubled the numbers. The message went through several local contacts – all equally helpful. So you can imagine our surprise – or horror – then, coming into the room expecting seven people to be faced with a crowd of about 50. Some group discussion!

The invitation needs to set out clearly the place and time as well as reassurance that the meeting is confidential and this is not a 'test' so they do not need to 'bone up' beforehand. In fact, to gain spontaneous views it is often better that they do not do so.

Draft invitation for participants in the XXX Focus Group

Dear XXX,

We want to ensure that our communication to our employees meets their needs. So we are organizing some discussion groups to talk about what works well and what does not and would like you to contribute to that discussion.

Meetings are being arranged with small groups of employees in different parts of XXX. We hope that you will be able to join the group discussion, which will take about an hour and a quarter.

At......................

In......................

The discussion will be informal – there are no right or wrong answers. You do not need to read up anything beforehand. It is completely confidential – your views will never be attributed to you as an individual.

We hope that you will be able to join us but if you are unable to do so, would you contact [local contact name here] as soon as possible.

Although you will need to give some indication of the objective of the discussion, you need not be too precise as to its content. For example, if the intent is to focus on the Intranet or internal publications, the overall purpose of the discussion could be outlined as communication. In this way, a spontaneous overview of internal communication and the context of the Intranet/publications can be gained before moving on to more specific questions.

- In certain cases, you may wish to do the opposite by asking the group to carry out some pre-tasks such as reviewing a publication or Intranet that may not have been read or accessed previously.
- There may be projects calling for specific groups of employees such as diversity or customer service where the participants will be chosen from that specific group to discuss these particular issues.

Organizing a suitable location

To create the right environment to put participants at ease and encourage them to speak out during a focus group, a relaxed, informal setting is needed, so a suitable location is important.

- Above all, they must feel they will not be overheard – I once carried out a group in a room where their manager came in every so often to 'make a cup of tea' – at least that was the excuse. So ensure there will not be any interruptions that may disturb the group.
- If there is no suitable room on the premises, a nearby hotel location is sometimes used. However, there is usually a training room or similar available. A word of warning, if the formal boardroom is used, this unaccustomed environment could be disconcerting for junior employees.
- Ensure that people are sitting reasonably close together – one of the qualitative interviewer's tasks is often to rearrange the room to ensure that people are not dotted apart around a large table – this inhibits participation, especially if one or two people are out on a limb.
- When organizing timings, remember to allow a half an hour or so between groups in case they run over and to give a chance for the facilitator to look over the notes. There may be points to highlight so they can be raised at subsequent groups. Impressions about the tone of the discussion and the general atmosphere are important – note these straight away to ensure your intuitive feelings are not forgotten when you come to put the material together towards the end of the project.

Developing a topic guide

Without any direction, a discussion may not cover all the points you wish to raise or provide focused feedback. A discussion or topic guide is precisely that – a guide for the discussion and the topics to be discussed. However, it should not be a straitjacket that disallows any spontaneous input. The topic guide needs to outline what you plan to cover:

- Introduction of facilitator and explanation of the purpose of the meeting/interview, its anticipated length and the fact that whatever individuals say will not be attributed to them personally or in any way that reveals their identity.
- Set out the ground rules – all should have an opportunity to participate, and explain that those who have much to say need to give everybody some time (which will make it easier if you need to silence those who have too much to say).
- Next, invite those present at a group to introduce themselves, or have paired introductions (which gives all present a chance to speak from the beginning) with how long they have worked there, what department. It may help to have place cards with their first names.
- Then you may want to introduce an ice breaker to relax the group. For example: if you had a magic wand that allowed you to change three work-related activities and you can change anything you want, how would you change yourself, your job, your boss, colleagues or a recent important project?
- When you move on to the discussion guide itself, start with the general before moving on to the specific.
- After each question, list some 'prompts' to ensure that you gain a reaction to specific points even if the group does not raise them. Or there may be probes of 'Why did you say that?' 'How did you feel?' 'Can you give a specific example?'
- At the end, remember to ask if there is anything else anybody wishes to raise before thanking them for their participation.

Sample discussion guide about organizational change

Introduction

Introduce self as the moderator of the group discussion. Explain that this is an informal discussion and confidential so nobody outside the room will know how people answered individually. Go round the table asking people to introduce themselves, how long they have worked there and where. Explain you have a discussion guide of points you wish to cover but you also want to hear about any issues that may not have been included.

General

- If somebody outside your organization asked you what is it like to work there, what would you say? (PROBE: As an employer and as a business. What do you like most? What do you like least?)

- When somebody asks where you work, what do you say? (PROBE: Name this organization? The market? Job function? Profession?)

- *Alternatively.* If this organization were an animal – what sort of animal would it be? (PROBE: Why do you say that?)

Aspects of working here

- Think about coming into work in the morning: what might happen to make it a great day for you? (PROBE: Your own work, behaviours of colleagues, manager.) Now think of a day when nothing seems to go right: what sorts of thing happen? (PROBE: Your job, colleagues, line manager.)

- Take the above points and discuss in more depth. Have others had the same experience? What could have been done to make a bad day good?

- Recent change? (PROBE: Formation of the proposed new team.) Impact generally – on service provided? On internal communication? (PROBE: Same? More? Less? Comfort with changes? Fully explained?)

Purpose/leadership

- Clarity of future direction? (PROBE: How communicated?)

- How well kept up-to-date about these changes? Specific department goals/plans?

- Leadership role? (PROBE: Behaviours? What do you see in practice? Positive behaviours? Negative behaviours?) (PROBE: Examples of these behaviours.)

Involvement

- How involved are you personally/team members in the changes? (PROBE: Examples.)

- Opportunities to be involved? (PROBE: Practical examples. How improved?)

Media

- From where do you get most of your information? (PROBE: List of main sources. Where did the information about change come from?)

- How useful do you find these personally? (PROBE: Why do you say that?)

Looking ahead

- What improvements (if any) would you like to see for the future? (PROBE: Practical examples.)

- If you were (suddenly) CEO here – what would be the first change/ improvement you would make? (PROBE: Any others.)

Finally: anything not covered in the discussion? **Thank for their contribution.**

Facilitating a meeting

This form of information gathering is non-numerical and puts the person facilitating the meetings in a key position. So it is not just a matter of listening to what people say, but also how they say it, words, tone and so on. You need to take an independent, neutral viewpoint, which can be difficult if you disagree with the comments. Observe non-verbal communication such as body language and voice intonation – this can reveal a great deal. Note at the time – it can be more difficult to recall afterwards when you have conducted a number of groups.

- External focus groups are often videoed or clients watch the discussion. This is not suitable for internal research where employees need to know that their views will not be attributed to them personally. If the topic is not sensitive or controversial then possibly it can be taped if this does not cause concerns about confidentiality. Otherwise, have a note-taker present, which can be useful as facilitator/note-taker roles can be reversed for subsequent meetings to share the lead discussion role and to give another viewpoint for interpretation. If you are a fast writer or do shorthand you may wish to make your own notes but this is less desirable as it is hard to listen actively as well as write.

- Clearly introduce yourself (and any note-taker) and give parameters for the meeting and refer to the topic guide to ensure that the discussion keeps to the subject in hand. However, do not slavishly follow the discussion guide – if an interesting comment is made, follow it up and return to the guide later.

- Listen carefully to what is said but don't lose control of the meeting. Stay impartial and don't get drawn into discussions/argument. It can be frustrating if people mention things that you know to be inaccurate but if you immediately correct them this could inhibit later discussion.

You could wait until a later stage if you want to get their reactions to the 'right' version. Some points can wait until the end of the meeting if you feel you must correct them.

- Manage the different types of people and ensure all have their say in some way – both Mr Mouse and Ms Shout-About.

- Mr Mouse will be the one who looks uncomfortable, keeps his head down, avoids eye contact and may not volunteer an opinion but mumbles if he does so. Quiet ones like this will also have a valuable contribution so ensure they are included. A shy person will not want attention drawn to them but you can use techniques to engage them. Try to establish eye contact and ask them directly what they think and whether they agree with what is being said. However, some people are naturally quiet and will remain so but once they have spoken out, they will find it easier to become involved. This is another reason why the initial 'warm up' is so important.

- At the other end of the spectrum is Ms Shout-About. She will always be the first to respond, interrupt her colleagues and talk, and talk and talk…. She speaks with authority and dominates the group. Often Ms Shout-About is not conscious that she is doing this and other members of the group will start to resent her dominance as speaking on their behalf and gradually quieten her naturally. If this does not happen, you will need to ensure that others have an equal say without being discourteous to the offender. You can avoid eye contact and address your question to the others. If the subtle hints do not work then you will need to be more direct and ask her to allow others their chance to speak to hear everyone's views.

- So watch for the group dynamics to encourage Mr Mouse and subdue Ms Shout-About. Some people do speak for the group, so watch other reactions – comments from one may be greeted with head nodding and general agreement.

- From time to time, summarize what has been said to ensure you understand what is meant and that you have captured the mood of the meeting.

- Keep the discussion focused but do not ignore comments that invite further probing – much valuable information could be lost by not following up issues where remarks made in passing are not covered in the discussion guide.

- Ensure your notes contain basics such as group numbers, timing, location, etc.

- Check future groups to reduce the number of no-shows.

- Build as you go – integrate some of the comments made in earlier groups to check on the perceptions of others and their reactions. 'Some of your colleagues have told us … why do you think they said that?'

- To keep the discussion live, get the group to move around from time to time – perhaps just changing places or using Post-it notes to put their thoughts on an ideas wall. Think of ways to involve them and make it easier to express their views. If the topic is change, have a chart with a line representing the change journey from start to finish, ask them where their organization is on that line, where they are and how they could be helped to move along the change line.

Projective techniques and exercises

These approaches can be used to help uncover feelings, motives and associations that may not be found through direct questioning. They range from asking people to complete a set sentence to showing a picture and asking what it represents. Completing a sentence could ask them to continue from: 'Today at work the best [worst] thing was ...'; finish this sentence thinking about you personally, your colleagues, and your boss. Or: 'The best thing that happened to me at work during the last week was...'. A favourite for internal research is to ask: 'If your organization was an animal, what would it be?' This can free people to suggest an elephant or a dinosaur when they may not wish to criticize directly. In one case, the board of a well-known food store that was facing problems looked ever more depressed as they heard the list of animals their managers had described, ranging from an extinct dodo to a dormant dormouse. Then a tiger was mentioned – a flutter of interest, this sounded better, until the full description expanded into a 'tiger with a wounded paw'. However, the message certainly got through.

Projective techniques are more frequently used for external research as internally, employees often have strong feelings that they are prepared to express clearly and openly without such stimulation. In cases where nebulous, sensitive aspects are researched – such as culture or brand – it may be useful to include such approaches.

Another technique is Appreciative Inquiry, an approach that looks for success stories rather than problems. It focuses on what works well and builds on strengths and asks 'What is the best we can be?' If this approach is adopted, it needs to be communicated at the start of the meeting, so participants know its purpose and do not think that any criticisms are just being ignored.

Appreciative Inquiry expert, Sue Derby, became a keen advocate of this approach during her time as director of internal communication at Xerox Canada. She is co-founder of Clockwork Communication based in Toronto and specializes in appreciative inquiry (AI). She explains that this is an action-based research approach developed in the early 1980s by David Cooperrider, Case Western Reserve University:

> As a collaborative search to identify and understand an organization's strengths, potentials, greatest opportunities, and people's hopes for the future, it has

become an increasingly popular approach for engaging employees, strategic planning and tackling complex organizational issues. While there are many ways to apply the philosophy, the most common model that describes the core processes of AI is the 4-D model – Discovery, Dream, Design and Destiny.

Another interactive approach is also becoming popular: impact or action workshops are involving employee groups to consider and suggest ideas, suggestions and solutions to business and people issues. These may call for participants to consider options, break out into smaller groups and come together to agree a way forward. Sometimes described as co-creation, this is a productive way to involve people in working together to create new ideas and develop solutions.

Telling a story ...

When time is too short to gather groups together or people are scattered – perhaps geographically, perhaps home workers or because they have left the organization – a series of stories can tell the tale.

An interview can elicit not just facts and figures but insights – there may only be 10 or 12 such interviews, usually by telephone, so this approach may not be entirely representative. However, the depth of information gained can be just as valuable. This can be turned into an individual story – provided, of course, that no specific information can tie the outcome with an individual as it is vital to preserve individual anonymity here.

Within these parameters, the feedback can describe the person and their reactions to the questions about their circumstances. In one case, this worked particularly well for people who had left this organization, giving the opportunity to understand the reasons in depth together with examples of incidents/ treatment that led to the decision to leave.

Interpreting and presenting the feedback

The group discussions/interviews are over and you are faced with piles of notes. This can be a despairing moment: how to turn these into a meaningful narrative and identify action points.

- Take your time – read the notes or listen to the tapes several times and underline or note the key points made and highlight any direct quotes to include in any report/presentation. Brainstorm with yourself.
- If this is a team project, brainstorm with the others to draw out main themes. If you were the only facilitator, you may be on your own, which can be difficult with a mass of material. Here Post-its or flow

charts can be helpful so the input can be considered and easily moved around as more themes emerge.

- You won't get always get consensus, so represent minority views and remain independent – it is about their views, not yours.
- At the same time you will need to summarize themes, seek relationships and draw conclusions from this mass of words to produce findings that relate to the purpose of the research that can be used for action planning.
- A feedback session can be more effective than a written report as this gives the opportunity for the audience (senior or department managers) to ask questions about particular findings so these can be explored in more depth in discussion notes and reported back.

Remember

- Appreciate that focus groups and interviews need effective facilitation and are not just general talking sessions.
- Think about using projective techniques to gain deeper understanding.
- Take plenty of time when reviewing the feedback and putting together a presentation or report so it can be used to direct a way ahead.
- Use focus groups and in-depth interviews for insights into 'subtle' topics such as mission and values.

Lies, damned lies and statistics

05

Don't just avoid this chapter – here's a basic guide to the three essential points to interpret results reliably for credible evidence-based decision making.

Why have these words stuck to statistics ever since Mark Twain uttered them? It is more accurate to define statistics as 'a branch of mathematics for analysis, evaluation and interpretation of numerical data.' They are integral parts of the research process and needed, both to gain better value from the data and to ensure that your findings can be trusted. However, when giving training courses I notice that when we come to this subject, people's eyes usually glaze over. I do have some sympathy. In my days as communication manager I was disappointed to find that rating of the house journal I edited had fallen by one point. No reassurance that this was not a significant reduction could convince me: rating had worsened in my eyes.

Now I know better: to ensure your actions are the right ones, you need to be certain that your information is reliable. This chapter cannot turn you into a statistician: statistics is a science and the amateur researcher cannot hope to match the knowledge and experience of the professional. The qualified statistician can carry out a variety of tests on your data – even one called the Kolmogorov–Smirnov test. These tests use a wide range of modelling and pattern-making tasks otherwise hidden in a sea of numbers. These include correlation (measuring the association between two variables) regression (measuring the association between one variable and others) and cluster analysis (grouping into categories, widely used for prediction and forecasting).

Do not abandon all hope at this stage. You do not need to become a statistician yourself to become familiar with the principles of statistics and understand their role in your research process. It is important to arm yourself with sufficient information about what makes results reliable and robust to ensure the hard quantitative data can be used for investment/resourcing decisions and not just dismissed by others as untrustworthy.

So what do you really need to know about statistics for conducting organizational research? There are three main things to keep in mind:

- the range of statistical tools available and their value;
- how to draw the correct conclusions about your results;
- what needs to be borne in mind to ensure that valid samples are drawn.

Before looking at each of these in turn, a question: What do terms such as statistical reliability and the law of probability mean in practice? How can you be sure that your data results are not based on chance? To answer this, one of the leading statisticians working in market research, Ken Baker, suggests a novel test to show how it works.

'Shuffle a pack of cards like mad,' says Ken, 'then take the first 10 cards off the top and note how many are hearts. This simulates the one sample you have made to estimate the proportion of hearts in a pack of cards. Now repeat this exercise taking 10 cards 99 more times, always shuffling the cards well. I will predict you will get the following results – predicted on the laws of probability.'

0 Hearts	–	4 times
1 Heart	–	17 times
2 Hearts	–	30 times
3 Hearts	–	28 times
4 Hearts	–	15 times
5 Hearts	–	5 times
6 Hearts	–	1 time
7+ Hearts	–	Not at all

'The average number of hearts over your 100 samples,' he points out, 'will be close to 2.5 or 1 in 4, which is the true population proportion. Very few of the answers will be at the extremes. Try it and see for yourself.'

He adds: 'Note that only five of the observations are at the extremes. Ninety-five of the observations are clustered reasonably close to the population average, usually known as the mean. This sort of distribution of results leads to the calculation of 95 per cent confidence intervals discussed below.'

Convinced? Now read on ...

Range of statistical tools

There is a wide range of statistical tools available to give deeper insight into the quantitative research results. If you want to know more, you will probably need the help of a statistician – if working with an external agency this advice should be part of the service (you could specify this in your brief). If you are conducting your own research internally you may wish to consult a statistician – your local market research society or ESOMAR, the world research organization which is represented in 100 countries, are good contact points here while the chapter on Statistics and Significance Testing by Paul Harris and Ken Baker in the *ESOMAR Research Handbook* gives an excellent overview. There are also sites online specializing in giving statistical advice that can be very useful.

Statistical reliability

During election times, you may have seen reports of political surveys among the general population, often in the small print stating that in the 1,000 sample, the findings will be 95 per cent correct within three percentage points. So if, say, 60 per cent hold a certain view, the actual figure could be 57 per cent or 63 per cent. The small print in some of the media is because what is trumpeted as a major change may not be statistically reliable, but why spoil a good headline?

However, from your viewpoint, for research among employees, it is essential to draw the correct conclusions about:

- The statistical reliability of the overall results (how close is this to the 'real' result if all had answered?).

- Track change over time (have our results improved or worsened?).

- Which differences between the results of various employee groups are 'real' (does department X really differ from department Y?).

Taking statistical reliability into account is an essential part of the research process to ensure your results are robust and reliable to reflect the actual situation in your organization and draw valid conclusions from the data. Imagine that you have received the results of your research and the CEO questions how reliable these are. By familiarizing yourself with these points you will be able to give a convincing answer, important during conversations with highly numerate corporate decision makers and programme managers, particularly when decisions are made about resource allocation.

To start with a basic fact: if everybody in the organization had participated in the research, then you could be sure that the results were 100 per cent reliable. However, this is unlikely to be the case: even if the research is a census rather than a sample, not all will have taken part. So how confident can you be that the overall results are really reliable? I was once informed firmly by a communicator as a fact that if at least 30 per cent of employees participate then you can be sure the results are accurate. Would that it were that simple!

For most external areas of research only a very small proportion of the universe is selected to participate. So in this case what you need to work out to assess how confident you can be in the reliability of a result, is the actual number of people who responded, not the percentage they represent. Another factor to take into account is the percentage answer rating they give. So if, for example, 500 people gave approval rating of 70 per cent to their team meetings, the chances are 95 in 100 that this figure would not vary more than about four percentage points (which is the confidence interval or margin of error). Thus if all employees had participated, the 'real' figure would be between 66 per cent and 74 per cent but is likely to be close to the midpoint. Here are some more examples.

- If 100 people give an approval rating to their team meetings at either the top or low end of the scale (around 10 per cent or around 90 per cent), the 'real' figure would be plus or minus 6 per cent (which is the margin of error here). If their response is around the midpoint (50 per cent) the reliable figure would be plus or minus 10 per cent (the margin of error) so we can infer with 95 per cent confidence that the 'real' figure would be between 40 per cent and 60 per cent.

- If 500 people responded, the plus or minus difference would reduce: at the two ends of the scale (around 10 per cent or 90 per cent) then the difference would need to be at least three per cent to be a reliable difference. At around 50 per cent, the difference needs to be at least four per cent.

- With 1,000 responses, the results become even more reliable. At around the two ends of the scale (around 10 per cent or 90 per cent) the difference needs to be two per cent for reliability and at around 50 per cent, a difference of three per cent.

So the more people who have responded, the smaller the confidence interval/ margin of error and the more reliable the results in statistical terms. Table 5.1 gives an indication of results reliability.

TABLE 5.1   Confidence intervals, or margins of error, for different sample sizes

Your sample size	Percent differences needed for 95% reliability at around these scores		
	10% or 90%	30% or 70%	50%
	+ or −	+ or −	+ or −
100 responses	6	9	10
300 responses	4	5	6
500 responses	3	4	4
1,000 responses	2	3	3

These figures may be different for employee research when a high response rate will represent a large proportion of the people in the organization. So, the higher the response rate, the lower the error, making the results more reliable. You may find Table 5.2 useful when working out the reliability of your results. These multipliers can be applied to the confidence intervals in Table 5.1 to take into account the numbers of employees who participated.

TABLE 5.2 Response rate multipliers for employee research

Response rate	Multiplier
10%	1.0 (ie no change from the percentages in Table 5.1)
25%	0.9
50%	0.7
75%	0.5 (ie the percentages in Table 5.1 would be halved)
100%	0.0 (ie a census, meaning the results reflect all)

Thus in this example, if 50 per cent of employees had taken part, giving 300 responses with an answer of 50 per cent in response to a question, the original confidence interval of plus or minus six per cent would be reduced to 6×0.7, making the confidence interval plus or minus four per cent.

If all this seems 'too complicated' remember that any action based on results that are not showing real differences will be wasted and could even cause harm rather than good.

Next, turning to looking at the results in more depth, how can we know there is a real difference between the overall total and one particular employee group? This sort of information is often used for action planning to identify those areas of best practice and also those below average or between different groups, such as managers and non managers, to see if the manager population is more positive and therefore able to act as leaders in a change programme.

Difference between the overall total and one employee group

Ken Baker gives this as an example: 'If you have replies from 45 out of a total population of 50 managers and 60 per cent of those managers thought the firm was "going in the right direction", you will want to know how this compares to the workforce average. Are the managers more or less positive about the future? Here the "real" figure will be plus or minus five per cent so the manager results will be between 55 per cent and 65 per cent (but it is most likely to be at the midpoint, 60 per cent). Next you will need to look at the non-manager results at 48 per cent. Even taking the sampling error into account (that 48 per cent could theoretically be as high as 53 per cent) this still shows that the manager results are significantly more positive by at least seven points.

So what does this mean for your understanding of the data? The main lesson is to understand that with small numbers of participants you need quite large differences between two sets of results to be sure their views really are different. Significance testing is a highly specialized subject and this chapter can only touch on it in terms of what you need to know for internal research. If you are working with an external agency, then tables showing a range of differences may be provided with the report to give you an accurate idea of the statistically significant differences. See Table 5.3.

TABLE 5.3   The impact of sample sizes on the statistical significance of results

Two sample sizes	Percentage differences		
	10% or 90%	30% or 70%	50%
	+ or −	+ or −	+ or −
100 and 100	8	13	14
100 and 200	7	11	12
500 and 500	4	6	6

These calculations will be particularly helpful when looking at change over time, from survey to survey or when drawing a valid sample. Some studies take a sample of 100 employees monthly as a temperature check. Indeed this is useful to keep in touch with workforce opinion but dangerous to use as an accurate gauge of change – a difference of more or less than 14 per cent on a 50 per cent rating is needed to indicate a reliable change.

One organization doing a regular monthly survey among a small sample went on a rollercoaster of action. The second month they were disappointed to find satisfaction with one aspect had dropped by five points – more effort was put into this with no apparent effect while another aspect that had not received any attention suddenly shot up 10 points. It took a few months to realize that the perceived ups and downs were meaningless – it was chance rather than a real change.

All of this may sound extremely complicated, especially to those of us who tend to be right-brained. But there is help in the form of a very useful online calculator to work this out for you: http://www.surveysystem.com/sscalc.htm.

If you want to calculate for yourself, the standard error of a percentage has a formula. It is the square root of:

$$\frac{p \times (100 - p)}{n}$$

where p is the answer percentage and n is the sample size. Thus if you have a 40 per cent answer for a question and the sample size is 1,000, the standard error is 1.55 and the 95 per cent confidence intervals lie in the range 40 per cent plus or minus three per cent. So we can be 95 per cent certain that the true value of p (ie the answer percentage) lies in the range 37 per cent to 43 per cent.

Valid samples

'Should we be carrying out a census or a sample?' is a frequent question followed by 'How big should my sample be?' There is no instant answer and you will need to take a number of considerations into account including statistical reliability.

A census will invite all employees to participate. This approach, which is certainly the best option for smaller companies, will:

- involve everybody throughout the organization, emphasizing that all contributions are valuable;
- make it easier to publicize and send reminders as all are included;
- provide (depending on response rates) sufficient numbers to reliably analyse specific employee groups and departments.

In the days before online surveys, the reason for deciding on a sample rather than a census in large organizations was usually the cost of print and data processing. Nowadays, where employees have online access, this is less relevant as numbers participating make little difference to online collection as respondents are inputting their own data.

However, you may need to consider a sample where large numbers are in retail, manufacturing or logistics without easy online access; where the subject matter does not call for a project involving large numbers of employees; or when regular research is needed without asking the same people on numerous occasions.

- When deciding the size of the sample, the desired reliability of the data needs to be taken into account. So rather than choosing an overall sample number to give reliable overall figures – say 1,000 representing one in 10 of the 10,000 strong workforce – you will need to work out each employee group where reliable results are needed for action planning. Thus if results by the office in Bristol with 50 people is needed, the one in 10 will only provide a sample of five – insufficient for analysis. (The best practice employee research 'rule of 10' should apply – that is commitment not to analyse groups smaller than 10 people, as recommended by the Market Research Society.)

- Consider carefully the groups where results will be needed and build up your sample size based on the numbers you want to achieve by each sub-group – location, department, function and so on. So if you want to look at managers in each department you will need to work this out. A sample of one in 10 across the whole organization may produce about nine managers per department – insufficient for robust separate results. Therefore to achieve sufficient numbers among this group, while the overall sample may comprise one in 10 you can invite all managers to take part. Of course, this means that the total results will over-represent the manager views and potentially misrepresent overall employee opinion.

- If the manager population is actually 10 per cent of the workforce but they form 20 per cent of the total research results, that needs to be down-weighted to reflect their actual proportion of the entire workforce to give a more accurate total.

- To draw a representative sample in a diverse organization you may also have to over-sample in certain groups (eg ethnic minorities) – this may be complicated and time-consuming so, if it is practical, you may find that the census is your most practical option rather than a sample.

Management often ask for a sample rather than involving the whole organization, under the impression this will be easier; so the above points are useful to point out the implications of this approach on the reliability of the results on which decisions will be based.

If the above chapter has given you a thirst for more information about statistics there are courses run by market research societies on this topic, among others, while various web pages give more background. Recognizing the need for a simple guide to statistics, the charitable trust Sense About Science in collaboration with the Royal Statistical Society has a downloadable guide from www.senseaboutstatistics.org.

So don't be a 'Squealer' – the pig in *Animal Farm* who used misleading statistics to 'prove' his case. Or, as the saying goes, 'use statistics as a drunkard uses a lamp post – for support, rather than illumination.' Please be among those who use statistics for illumination!

Remember

- Learn about the value the range of statistical tools can provide.
- Be aware of your results validity with statistical reliability tests.
- Consider what size your samples should be to gain robust results.
- Make sure you can answer confidently if the reliability of the results is questioned.
- Look at the ways external research uses segmentation and other techniques that could also be used internally.

Conversation 3
Learn from external research techniques and take a holistic view: **Sandra Macleod**, group CEO, Echo Research

Research among customers, consumers and key stakeholders externally uses a wide range of statistical techniques to better understand those various groups, to learn how they differ from one another. Who is more likely to buy a product, for example, or where there is a group with an unmet need. This learning can then be applied to create targeted messaging and media plans, to set new business strategies, or bring new products to market. There is potential to use similar techniques internally. External and internal research are often seen as separate entities but not for Sandra Macleod who heads Echo Research, a global specialist in reputation analysis and stakeholder research. She also feels that both internal and external communication are inextricably linked. 'The message needs to be the same to all audiences, although the delivery may be different,' she points out.

Sandra is a strong advocate of taking a holistic view of strategic communication and hence providing value to the organization. The challenge is to bring the two sides of communication together effectively. Both need to be embedded into the organizational strategy, according to Sandra, who points out that the communication should not just be a bolt on: 'Look closely at the whole entity of the organization – there are often too many silos: marketing, advertising, PR, HR and communication – these barriers need to be broken down,' she urges, 'we need more joined up thinking.'

She is also a strong believer in Key Performance Measures to drive communication performance by developing numerical measures of outputs and outcomes of communication channels and messages. 'Measurement and evaluation are essential in the creation of successful communication programmes for your various stakeholder groups,' she explains.

'Among those important stakeholders are your employees; how they perceive your organization and whether you communicate sufficiently with them can have a direct effect not only on your communication programme but also your organization's ability to reach its strategic objectives,' Sandra says. It is also vital to remember that your employees are more influenced by what they see in the 'objective' outside media, most often in social media from their peers and trusted sources, to a far greater extent than the news the official internal channels carry.

She explains that content analysis of the external and social media helps answer questions such as: What is the connection with your brand through these channels? How consistent, coherent or disconnected is it from what you want to communicate? What are the strong signals you should address swiftly and the weak signals your radar should be alert to? What are the ecosystems of influence you should know about and manager better?

The effectiveness of this kind of analysis is shown by the extent to which it helps uncover trends in the message reach, any changes in opinion-formers' positions, and shifts in reading/recalling messages and materials among audience groups. Drawing these elements together into a cohesive picture of message, source, influence, medium and audience gives valuable insights to shape your communications strategy so that it is truly aligned both inside and outside the organization.

Until recently, such research approaches for public relations, reputation and stakeholder research have been more sophisticated and wide-ranging than those used internally. However, best practice for external communication research shares many of the tools, techniques and approaches with internal research.

'Look at your internal media in the same way,' advises Sandra. 'For example, how frequently is your audience exposed to your organizational messages, how often are they accessed, is there a gap between the messages and how they are understood?' Are these at odds or consistent with what they are exposed to elsewhere? Using any existing external research can provide further insights: most internal communication tends to take a positive slant, but if analysis of tone of voice in the outside media reveals a mainly negative impression, then employees will be receiving mixed and confusing messages.

So Sandra's counsel is to take into account existing research into your organization's reputation and media and digital coverage, as well as making use of its techniques when measuring and evaluating internal communication. 'Above all, take a holistic view,' she says, 'study and understand the management strategy to ensure that your communication – both internal and external – is embedded fully into that strategy to better build resilience and, above all, trust, which is so essential to engagement and effort.'

Questionnaire development and design

06

H ere we look at the steps to develop a balanced and objective questionnaire that reflects the needs of the business.

This well-known saying has real resonance: Asking a silly question brings an equally silly answer. Or perhaps: Asking a leading question brings a misleading answer. The output of the research is dependent on the input, so an effective questionnaire must be clear, relevant to the audience and unbiased. Questionnaire design is influenced by whether it is paper, online or telephone, but whichever approach you use you will need to consider:

- A covering letter or note with the questionnaire to communicate the purpose of the survey, closing time for returns and any clear instructions and relevant information to help with questionnaire completion; for example, whether 'organization' refers to the individual company or group. This clarity is essential to ensure there is no ambiguity when considering the feedback. It is also an opportunity to communicate the value of each person's contribution, when they can expect to see the results and commitment for action planning.

- Content must reflect the needs of the research and the business. Space is too precious to waste on irrelevant topics. What information will be obtained from each question and how will it be used? Nice to know does not cut it here – every single question must be need to know.

- There should be a logical flow with general, easier to answer questions first, leading on to more complex issues. Although similar topics should be grouped together (eg human resource aspects such as training, development and appraisal) it can be counterproductive to put these clearly under section headings as this may lead the respondent to answer in a certain way, influenced by that heading. Sometimes there is a temptation to divide questions under values or mission sections if this is the purpose of the research. However, remember that you can group responses together under these headings at the later results stage – they need not be clustered together here.

- Questions can be open – where the respondent writes in their own words – or closed – either multiple choice where a number of options can be selected from a list or single choice where only one answer is sought.

- Language needs to be understandable to the audience so management jargon must be avoided. Some years ago before the phrase became well known, an employee told me seriously that he had heard that senior management had 'seen a vision'. When another saw the word 'integrity', she responded, 'pass me the dictionary'.

- Wording must be objective to avoid receiving the obvious answer. It is possible to lead people to answer in a certain way: this should be avoided.

- This was shown when two statements were once given as (bad) examples to illustrate this point at a talk. One said: 'Selfish landowners must not stop people walking on the land that should belong to all.' The other: 'Careless people who could harm the countryside must not be allowed on private land.' To our amazement, there was agreement with both statements – although they reflect opposite views – thus demonstrating the power of strongly worded leading questions to influence responses.

- Each question should contain one concept, otherwise it will not be clear to which the response refers. 'Communication here is open and timely.' Which will their answer refer to – employees might feel it is open but not timely and vice versa. However, there will be some concepts that do belong together: 'communication here is open and honest', for instance.

- Where scales are used they must be balanced. A five-point scale with a mid-point is often used – an unbalanced scale brings unbalanced results.

- To give another example: a media report about employee motivation levels gave a much higher figure than the average we had encountered at MORI. I contacted the researchers to try and ascertain the reason for the discrepancy. At first this was a mystery – respondent profile, timing, nothing seemed to explain the difference. However, when I asked about the scale I learned this was actually four points – described as 'excellent', 'very good', 'good' and 'poor'. So, three positive options and one negative, no wonder their finding was higher – and inaccurate.

- The balanced five-point scale, known as the Likert scale, may have a label for each: 'strongly agree' to 'strongly disagree'. Alternatively, respondents can be asked to give a rating with five as 'to a great extent' down to one 'not at all' with three at the midpoint. There is an argument for using the 'finer' 10-point scale, especially as people are often asked for marks out of 10 so this may be more familiar to them. Some may dislike choosing an extreme point on the shorter scale (five or one) so a 10-point scale gives a wider range of options and thus a broader spectrum of responses. This scale can be more appropriate for a multi-cultural study where some cultures are less likely to criticize their organization so may plump for the top score of five whereas the wider scale gives them the opportunity to score eight or nine, which may more accurately reflect their views.

- There is a school of thought that argues that respondents should be forced to make a choice rather than take the easy option of a 'don't know' or 'no opinion' or just do not care. This is a misconception. If employees really do not hold a view one way or another they must be allowed to express this uncertainty. Otherwise they could be forced to come down one side or the other at random, skewing the results.

- I emphasize that these 'don't knows' are a very important group. They are not yet positive or negative but sitting on the fence as they have insufficient information to make a choice. Those holding a negative view will be difficult to move into the positive. Fence sitters are a great opportunity – they will be open to listening about that subject so they can make an informed choice next time.

- Avoid row after row of agree/disagree statements – they become boring and the respondent might not think about each carefully but go into automatic mode, just ticking one column to give the same answer.

- Don't ask people to rank answers from a list – it can be difficult and time-consuming for the respondents. The results will show X per cent chose this as one, X per cent as two and so on, which may not give the clear priorities you seek. By asking respondents to tick as many as apply, the percentage results here will show the relative order of each. If you need to know the top one, then a subsequent question can ask them to select their first choice from that list.

- If you are uncertain that all options are included in a list, then 'other' or 'none' needs to be an additional choice. But do not select this as an easy escape from an exhaustive list – those writing in 'other' will need to be put into categories, which is time-consuming.

- I have seen questionnaires with numerous open questions inviting people to write in responses in their own words. This may seem an ideal solution to gain rich data. However, it generates masses of material that will need to be coded to gain a sense of the strength of opinion. This is slow and expensive: if so much spontaneous feedback is needed then focus groups could be the answer. However, to omit any opportunity for employees to give unprompted feedback is a mistake.

- At least one open question should be included to ensure that no major points have been left out and to show respondents that you are not just forcing them to keep to a pre-determined agenda.

- There may also be other questions where further input is required. Where people give a negative response to a certain question, you may wish to follow up with a 'Why do you say that?'

- Reading through all responses will provide some interesting quotes to bring the research alive. However, to gain an overall impression of strength of feeling, they need to be coded into categories with common themes.

- If you are using an external agency, a professional coder will carry out this task. To reduce costs, you may wish to ask for a percentage to be coded rather than all responses.

- To carry out this task yourself you will need to develop a code frame. This comprises of looking through the first 50 or so and grouping them under main themes. Assign each a number then, when going through all the comments, code each with the relevant number that can then be totalled to summarize these main themes. Here is an example when the question asked for the best things about working for that company.

General mentions	Number of times	Code no
Like the people/friendly/good colleagues	/ / / / / / / / (8)	1
Good training/helpful courses/guides	/ / / / / / (6)	2
Good promotion prospects/able to get on	/ / / / / / (6)	3

So when all mentions within that category have been categorized or coded, all the different remarks can be summarized as:

The top three aspects of working here that people most liked were their colleagues and the friendly atmosphere (40 per cent), the good training (35 per cent) and the opportunity for progress/promotion (30 per cent).

- If this is a large-scale survey with many open questions, verbatim content management programmes are available to group these together. The set-up costs will be higher but could save time and expense in the long term.

- Routing – the advantage of an online or telephone questionnaire or interview is that you can 'route' questions. So if somebody gives a certain answer this gives the opportunity to ask a further relevant question. If they have attended a certain training course, for instance, the questionnaire can be routed for those people only to gain a rating, while those who did not attend will not see this particular question.

An integral part of the questionnaire will be the demographic section to record relevant information about each respondent so that analysis can show results for specific groups.

- This section is usually at the end of the questionnaire as people may find it less intimidating and intrusive rather than it being up front. However, if some questions are specific to employees' function or department, these will need to be at the beginning so the relevant questions can be aimed at the right people.

- Ask yourself what information is really needed – people can be concerned about identification ('I am the only assistant manager aged 30–35 in Bristol') so only ask these personal details if they will be used. In practice, such information is often gathered but unused. Also include a note to explain that there will be no separate analysis of individuals or groups less than 10.

- The demographics may include department, role level, location, function, service length, age and other characteristics such as customer-facing. You should explain clearly why this information is needed, as in the example below.

Employee survey – about you

These questions are not intended to identify you individually. Much of the value of listening to your views will be to hear what you say within your own group of colleagues – for example, your job level. This is the reason for this section about you. Please be assured that – even if you are the only person who would fit into all the categories you complete – nobody's individual views will ever be shown separately. We keep to the rules of the Market Research Society not to analyse groups of staff under 10 in number.

- With the growing focus on diversity, many questionnaires also ask about ethnicity and sexual orientation. This can be a double-edged sword as some will resent such personal questions while others want their views represented within these specific groups. An explanation of why this information is wanted helps here, as many organizations now have diversity targets.

- Asking about nationality or geographic location as well as ethnicity needs to be approached sensitively. If you are intending the questionnaire for a UK or US sample, then basing any ethnicity question on the census categories could be more suitable. If elsewhere, local census categories may be appropriate, while careful consideration needs to be given as ethnic categories may be described differently. Advice can be sought from your local offices.

Having developed and designed your questionnaire, the next stage is to test it with several employee groups before going live. You ignore this piloting step at your peril. A great deal of thought and consultation will have already gone into its formulation so any further changes may not be welcome. However, you will still need to try out the questionnaire for relevance to its audience, time taken for completion and comprehension.

- Along similar lines to focus groups, ask several groups at different levels to complete the questionnaire. Note how long this takes and whether, having completed it, there is anything that they feel has been missed out.
- Next, was there anything unclear or difficult to answer?
- Finally, go through question by question checking on each that it is not causing problems or mistakes. If you have concerns about some items, you can ask what they understood by that wording, etc.

No matter how well your questionnaire has been researched and designed, there will be some aspects that will need to be revised. A typical misunderstanding relates to who is meant by 'my manager' and this may need to be more explicit; ie the person who does your appraisal. In one example, it became clear there was a problem with the job level: the HR department who provided the list believed Level One meant top management – only when some shop floor people filled in the form as Level One did we discover that this level was also a definition in the factory. As you can imagine, if this had not been clarified, the feedback for these groups would have been mixed and thus meaningless.

It is very easy for management jargon to slip in, together with words that may seem obvious to us, but not to those completing the questionnaire. Sometimes the feedback is surprising – but telling. In one instance in a scale the word 'rarely' caused problems – it was just not understood – and had to be replaced with 'seldom'.

One question that often arises is how long should the questionnaire be or how many questions should it contain. It is not so much the number of questions as the time taken to complete; some questions are more complex to consider than others, needing more thinking time. Counting the number of times a response is needed – that is the number of 'clicks' or 'ticks' the respondent makes can be a useful way of determining length. Remember, one question may have several parts, each asking for responses.

- For a workforce unaccustomed to questionnaires, with a high proportion of part-timers or shop-floor people, a short questionnaire with about 50 responses and around 10-minute timing should be a good indicator.

- Where a higher response rate can be expected, a timing of up to a quarter of an hour or 100 responses is about right.

- In an organization where people are accustomed to working online or writing, then 20 minutes or so plus 120–40 responses should not be a problem.

- The research subject will also be an influence: if it relates to something that is not seen as a strong part of working life (the company journal, for instance) there will be a lower response than an employee survey that may cover personal development, performance feedback and other aspects dear to the hearts of the people.

With input from several sources and eagerness to cover as much as possible, the questionnaire can become rather like the rolling stone that gathers moss. Resist at all costs – research shows that when people become fed up with the time taken in finishing the questionnaire, their responses become less thoughtful and possibly more inaccurate. And, of course, there is the final verdict – they just abandon your questionnaire altogether....

Although the content is of prime importance, the design and look of the questionnaire itself also plays a part in attracting participation. Here there needs to be a balance. A printed questionnaire that looks expensive can be a turn off, suggesting excessive expenditure, while cheap-looking versions with boring lists of questions tightly fitted on a page can be off-putting, suggesting a cheap approach. An online version needs to be easy and quick to navigate otherwise respondents lose patience. Web-hosting agencies often put a bar at the top of the page so that respondents can see how far they have reached as they progress.

Now the questionnaire is in peak position – it is time to send it out to its audience.

Remember

- Ensure that your questionnaire is balanced and relevant.
- Make it easy to complete, without management jargon.
- Check there are no double meanings that could be misinterpreted.
- Test and revise as required before going live.

Conversation 4
Agree to disagree:
Peter Hutton,
founder of BrandEnergy Research

Employee survey questionnaire design has gone off in completely the wrong direction according to Peter Hutton, author of *What Are Your Staff Trying to Tell You? Revealing the Best and Worst Practice in Employee Surveys*. His beef is the agree/disagree scale. Most employee surveys these days, he contends, consist almost exclusively of a list of statements, with staff asked to indicate how strongly they agree or disagree with each one. This, says Peter, results in questionnaires that provide partial and misleading information that can send management off in completely the wrong direction.

'You don't get this blinkered obsession with one question technique in any other area of research,' points out Peter, who has worked in many, including market research and opinion polling.

> Imagine someone giving directions and all they could do was respond by saying whether they agreed or disagreed with statements you put to them. It could take you some time to get to the answer you want and you would probably miss out on a lot of other really useful information that could have been elicited if you were not constrained by how you could ask the questions.

While he accepts that you cannot ask questions in surveys in the same way as you might in a normal conversation, he claims that you should be able to call on the full range of question techniques available to the researcher rather than just one type of scaled question.

The technique has been around for many decades and was developed to provide a way of measuring people's attitudes and opinions. Its attraction for employee research consultants is that you can dream up a statement about almost any subject and put it into your questionnaire. But that does not necessarily make it the best way to ask the question, says Peter.

> Often it is not even the best way to measure attitudes and opinions. If you want to know how useful staff find different forms of communication, like team meetings, why ask them whether or not they agree or disagree that 'team meetings are useful'? It is far better to use a usefulness scale (eg 'very useful' to 'not at all useful') and take the opportunity to ask about the other main channels to provide context.

Being able to see things in context rather than have a long list of what Peter calls 'one dimensional measures,' he suggests, is a key drawback of the technique.

> Suppose you wanted to find out which channels of communication staff used most. Asking them how strongly they agreed or disagreed that 'I use the staff newsletter most for finding out about what is going on in the company' is highly subject to error because you are not providing any comparisons for staff to choose from. Far better to present staff with a list of, maybe, a dozen items and ask which they use most often.

The technique also suffers from what Peter describes as the 'attitude conundrum'. One attitude, eg thinking that your manager does not care about you at work, could be the result of a whole host of issues that have nothing to do with the manager being uncaring – for example, through no fault of the manager, you may not have had a pay increase for five years. Moreover, one issue, eg not having had a pay increase for five years, can manifest itself in a whole host of attitudes most of which appear to have nothing to do with pay. The upshot is that many staff surveys generate a large number of measures of attitudinal symptoms but little insight into the underlying causes. Although the results may look highly actionable, they can actually send management spinning off in completely the wrong direction.

Peter also points out that as a technique designed to measure attitudes and opinions, he feels it is very poor at measuring other aspects of employee engagement and communication such as knowledge, behaviours and motivations.

> Imagine you wanted to find out how often your staff accessed the company Intranet. With the agree/disagree format you have to ask how strongly staff agree or disagree that they use the Intranet, what, Daily? Weekly? A lot?

A little? It is really much better to use a frequency scale which will give you the whole range of responses rather than just a limited impression.

The agree/disagree technique undoubtedly has its uses but in Peter's view it should be the technique of last resort: 'If you try all the other ways of asking questions and still conclude that the agree/disagree scale is the best way to elicit the information you really need, then fine, but nine times out of ten it isn't.'

Maximizing response rates

07

These are some of the tactics to encourage employees to take part by completing their questionnaires.

You have distributed your great questionnaire and are sitting back, waiting for the replies. Is all your hard work greeted with the sound of silence? Rather like organizing a party to which nobody turns up?

Your efforts will be wasted unless people participate. A low response rate provides unreliable data, which will certainly give those who may not wish to accept the results an easy way out. Senior management often ask about the opinion of those who do not respond, perhaps in the misguided hope that they represent the contented majority.

CASE STUDY 5 International Transport Workers' Federation: giving a voice to seafarers worldwide

Perhaps the greatest challenge to making contact with difficult to reach people to research their views came with the largest ever survey of seafarers' working conditions commissioned by the International Transport Workers' Federation and conducted by MORI back in 1996.

The ITF had been helping seafarers since 1896, working to improve conditions for seafarers of all nationalities and ensure adequate regulation of the shipping industry to protect the interests of the workers. An estimated 90 per cent of world trade uses maritime transport, depending on more than 1.2 million seafarers to operate the ships. Those seafarers – often working far from home – might be working on ships under a different flag from their origin or ownership. They might be exposed to difficult working conditions, at risk of accidents and work long hours. It was also known that they are vulnerable to exploitation and abuse, non-payment of wages, non-compliance with contracts, exposure to poor diet and living conditions, and even abandonment in foreign ports.

To address these issues, firm evidence was needed of seafarers' living conditions to reveal this situation and give a voice to seafarers. The union determined to gain that evidence by carrying out the first ever survey of seafarers worldwide so the conditions could be publicized and improved. However, a project like this faced a number of major challenges.

Development of the questionnaire was the easy part here. The difficulty was to get that questionnaire to the seafarers around the world and then receive them back. A significant proportion of the seafarers spoke a mixture of languages and experienced racial and even physical abuse. They could also be prevented from joining trade unions and it was recognized at an early stage that some ships' masters would not want – would even prevent – their crews completing questionnaires about their living conditions.

The language issue was overcome by translating the questionnaire into the relevant languages including Tagalog, the Austronesian language spoken mainly in the Philippines. But the main hurdle remained: how to get these questionnaires into the hands of the seafarers? The answer turned out to be perhaps the most unusual distribution method undertaken. ITF inspectors and chaplains working with seafarers were asked to help distribute and collect the questionnaires. In some ships, the masters welcomed the research but in others where the masters were less than willing, not to say positively antagonistic, the ITF inspectors had to distribute and collect the questionnaires secretly when they visited the ships in the various ports. Meanwhile, in the international seafarers' centres, the chaplains also gave out and collected the questionnaires.

The success of this approach was seen in the response when 6,500 replies came from 93 countries while seafarers on Flag of Convenience vessels (FOC) made up 44 per cent of those taking part in the survey, approximately the same proportion as gross tonnage of the world fleet. The number of responses, plus the worldwide coverage, ensured that the results of this survey of seafarers' living conditions were statistically reliable – an important point when publicizing the results.

'The survey revealed that over 70 per cent of all ratings were earning less than the ITF benchmark,' commented Mark Dickinson, then assistant general secretary of the ITF. This was at a time when the wages of the lowest paid often had to support five family members back home.

The results also showed that poor working conditions were not confined to Flag of Convenience fleets. Others came at the bottom of the league table for long hours, low pay and unsafe working conditions. An important link was seen between the number of hours worked and the level of accidents on board as well as between the long hours and high levels of stress and low morale.

Mark pointed out that everybody suffered from these conditions: 'not least those owners who are determined to uphold decent standards for the safe and efficient running of their vessels by a well-trained and fairly-rewarded crew.' All this evidence was invaluable to tackle the problems both with publicity and the role of the ITF inspectors in monitoring those ships and owners with the worst records. Mark Dickinson adds:

> The survey was used on many fronts to argue for better regulation in international shipping ... The Maritime Labour Convention 2006 became a regulation pillar of the

globalized shipping industry alongside training, safety and environment. Now we have social standards, too, and in no little part achieved by having that solid evidence from the seafarers themselves.

Today, the problems of making contact with seafarers have been transformed with communication via online systems. Recent research by the ITF Seafarers Trust surveyed 1,000 seafarers and revealed how they use modern communication technology from websites and email to SMS and social networking.

Onboard access to email has risen threefold since the Living Conditions survey took place – although nearly half do not have access on board, most do when they return home. Feelings of isolation are reduced as communication with family and friends has become stronger, with the opportunities for regular contact provided by mobile phones and SMS messages. Websites are a strong communication tool – 50 per cent of seafarers access the Internet at least twice a month while at sea, which rises to 80 per cent at home. Problems of seafarers' living conditions have not been completely resolved but new technology has given them a stronger voice.

How can you persuade people to give their time to fill in a questionnaire? Can you convince them that it is important enough to give their opinions?

To address this question, I carried out a small-scale survey, interviewing employees from three very different organizations face-to-face to find out why people had not participated in a questionnaire survey.

The prime reason was consistently the same: participation was seen as a waste of time – no action had followed previous research, so why should this time be different? There was also a range of other reasons from concern about personal anonymity to 'the dog ate the form'. However, the overall impression is that if there is an attitudinal bias among non-respondents, this is (unfortunately) more likely to be negative than positive.

Experience bears out the fact that where organizations had not been seen to address the issues raised in previous research proactively, response rates to subsequent questionnaires fell. However, in organizations that had listened to the feedback and reported-back action, response rates increased slowly but surely over time.

The three main ways to make a compelling case for action are:

- The CEO and senior management team must be seen to be fully behind the process. So an overt and genuine commitment from them to listen and take action where practical and possible is paramount. This last point is vital – expectations must be managed – this is not management by opinion poll.

- In turn, senior management commitment shows middle managers that the leadership – their bosses – value the process, meaning line managers will be more likely to encourage their people to take part; another prime way to gain high participation.

- And where action has happened, do not imagine that by a process of osmosis employees will recognize these changes. Continually publicize cases where survey feedback has guided communication and HR initiatives. A small Survey Action logo in print/online to signal any actions taken can tell your people that action stems from their feedback.

Other tips to stimulate response rates

- Ensure that the research programme is fully communicated: with a timetable and assurance that results will be shared with employees.
- Create a publicity campaign to build enthusiasm – where it fits with the company culture, this can be fun with posters and other teasers. Using a popular TV show such as the UK's *Strictly Come Dancing* as a theme could attract interest, as in these examples from designer Mick Upton.

FIGURE 7.1   Promotional poster for an upcoming survey (example 1)

Strictly Come Survey

make sure you send in your vote in our survey by this date

FIGURE 7.2   Promotional poster for an upcoming survey (example 2)

- Make the questionnaire simple and easy to complete (see Chapter 6).
- Questions must be relevant – the oft-quoted 'survey overload' only applies if the topics are irrelevant and unimportant to the audience.
- Reassure people that their responses will never be tied to them as individuals. Market research best practice suggests that small groups should not be analysed separately to ensure that they feel comfortable answering openly.
- Incentives or prizes are sometimes seen as a bright idea to stimulate responses. This has two drawbacks: people may respond for the wrong motives – just to be in a prize draw – and it is an inappropriate image for a survey with serious intent. They may even not respond honestly fearing identification, so results gained through prizes may not be accurate.
- One way to encourage participation is a donation to charity for each returned questionnaire or a set donation depending on the level of

responses. This is persuasive, but not tempting enough to just give positive answers.

- Communicate the response levels by location or team, so low-participation hot spots can be addressed quickly. Knowing that senior management will take a low response in their area seriously is a great persuasion for line managers to encourage their team to participate.
- Send a reminder – either emails or posters with the deadline date for returns – this does not usually make a major difference but does help those who may have forgotten.
- Make it clear that all are able to take company time to participate – and ensure that managers allow this, especially in target-driven areas such as call centres.
- Encourage but do not force: some organizations almost lock their people in a room until they complete the questionnaire. Yes, they can then boast about a high response rate – but what about the value and accuracy of responses from those forced to participate against their will?

And if you are successful what sort of response rate can you expect? Most returns come in the first few days of questionnaire distribution whether on paper or online. Typical response rates vary between type of organization and employee. In a retail environment with a high turnover and many part-timers, you might expect as low as 30–40 per cent. In an office-based organization, it could reach 80 per cent plus. On average, between 60 per cent and 70 per cent would be reasonable.

Remember

- Gain and communicate the commitment of the senior team and line managers.
- Reassure people about their individual anonymity.
- Communicate the purpose of the research, its findings, senior management response and practical examples of action undertaken.
- Recognize that during times of change and reorganization response rates are likely to decrease unless people are motivated to give their views.
- Where people are difficult to contact, try to find different ways to ensure a good response rate from those difficult to reach.

PART 2
Strategy
Insights to link your research to business success with engagement and high performance

Burning issues for your research to cover

08

We now move on to strategic issues, starting with three key areas where research can contribute towards stronger performance and organizational success: engagement, communication and change.

Looking back to the early days of internal research, much of its content and approach was informed by the Maslow Hierarchy of Needs, developed in the USA during the 1940s to 1950s. This showed five levels of human need: starting at the basic level, physiological needs (for food, water, etc); moving upwards to safety needs (security); and then on to the next level of love/belonging (family, friends); esteem (confidence, respect for self and others); and at the top, self-actualization (personal growth, confidence). Although this hierarchy of needs pyramid concept is still relevant today for understanding human motivation and personal development, research among employees is moving on from these foundations.

Traditional employee surveys tended to cover a 'little bit of everything'. This has proved useful in the past, but in today's fast-changing world there is a shift towards focusing in more depth on certain key topics to bring specific information and insights about the business and its people.

So what are the 'hot topics' for measurement? In this chapter we look at three of the burning issues currently topping the corporate agenda that are usually the subject of internal research, together with some suggested question areas to consider. First, we need to understand these will never be definitive – as our world constantly changes, so we must keep up-to-date with new ideas, issues and topics that become relevant for exploration. Thinker Daniel H. Pink, in his book *Drive*, recognizes three drives: the first the biological urge (similar to the basics of the Maslow needs); then comes what he describes as our 'reward and punishment drive'. This, he suggests, has become the conventional view of business motivation. However, he defines a third drive as the 'purpose' drive – that is the need to direct our own lives, to learn, create and improve things both for ourselves and our world. How many internal surveys truly investigate these drives in the lives of our colleagues? The closest we have come so far is the concept of employee engagement.

Engagement

One word, but a myriad of meanings and models. These sometimes clarify but can obscure 'engagement'. The whole area of engagement is one that has topped organizational agendas for the past few years but its definition takes many forms. Why are there so many definitions? Does that matter? Are we too hung up about its precise description?

It has been said that 'you'll know it when you see it'. This may be true but does not help when identifying what needs to be measured to assess the strength of employee engagement. Some form of definition and description is vital to identify what needs to be measured and this should be agreed to by the senior management as relevant and appropriate to their organization.

All too often the old employee survey is trotted out and renamed 'the engagement survey' while it is no such thing. This is why it is important to recognize that engagement is not another word for satisfaction. A satisfied employee may be that way because they do not feel pushed at work, they're paid well for what they do and never bother to do more than asked. So they may be very satisfied indeed. An engaged employee is quite different.

If you want to consider some of the many definitions of employee engagement you only have to surf the net to find dozens. Here is not the place to support one as 'the best' definition – there isn't one. The best definition will be what is right for your own individual organization. Here are just a few, some simple and direct, others more detailed:

- 'Employee engagement describes employees' emotional and intellectual commitment to their organization and its success. Engaged employees experience a compelling purpose and meaning in their work and give of their discrete effort to advance the organization's objectives' (The Work Foundation).

- 'Being positively present during the performance of work by willingly contributing intellectual effort, experiencing positive emotions and meaningful connections to others' (Kingston Business School Employee Engagement Consortium).

- 'A heightened emotional connection that an employee feels for his or her organization, which influences him or her to exert greater discretionary effort to his or her work' (The Conference Board).

- A founder of Engage for Change, John Smythe says that 'Engagement is delivered by a culture of distributed leadership, primarily through leaders at every level sharing power in a well-governed way which makes it safe for people at work to liberate their creativity to deliver surprisingly good results for their institution and for themselves.'

- In the USA, after a review of definitions across the market, Shelley Gable, freelance writer, summarized: 'An engaged employee is a high-quality performer who takes personal responsibility to work toward the success of the organization.'

So with all these definitions and descriptions how best to measure the level of engagement and – most importantly – direct initiatives and investment into the most effective channels? Every organization is individual, so models with one set of questions that claim to be all that is needed to measure engagement need to be treated with caution. It is worth spending some time reviewing the work that has already gone into understanding engagement and what it entails before moving to any measurement. Three good sources to inform and stimulate thinking are 'Engaging for success: enhancing performance through employee engagement', a report to government by David MacLeod and Nita Clarke, published in 2009; John Smythe's *The CEO: Chief Engagement Officer* (and *Velvet Revolution at Work: The rise of employee engagement, the fall of command and control*, due in January 2013); and the lively web engagement forum The Employee Engagement Network founded and hosted by David Zinger, now with 4,000-plus members. This lively website http:// employeeengagement.ning.com/ has great resources as well as an enthusiastic community sharing their experiences and ideas. Based in Canada, David says he fuses a prairie presence from Winnipeg to Warsaw and Wales and from Saskatchewan to San Antonio, Texas. David's 20/20 vision is to foster a 20 per cent global increase in employee engagement by the year 2020. 'I firmly believe this community will play a major role in that 20 per cent increase,' he says.

However, one hurdle to achieving this vision is the ever-increasing pace of change. Major changes bring major challenges to any organization but these can be overcome, as our case study shows when EDF Energy recognized the importance of taking their employees with them on a transition journey from their old world to the new.

CASE STUDY 6   EDF Energy: an energetic transition

One of the UK's major energy suppliers to domestic and commercial markets with 5.5 million customers, EDF Energy is part of a sector seeing continuous change since privatization over 20 years ago. A key part of Paris-based EDF group, EDF Energy has grown since its formation in 2001 through acquisitions and mergers, most recently British Energy with its eight nuclear power stations. In addition, EDF Energy has two coal-fired power stations, plans for four new nuclear plants and a large gas-fired plant and is expanding its wind-generation capacity.

With this forthcoming change journey in mind, there was recognition that 'opinion' – just finding out employee attitudes through its regular employee surveys – was no longer enough. The focus needed to be engagement to involve and mobilize its people. This needed to be managed and supported throughout the process to ensure ownership and action within the organization. A central role was created to be responsible for keeping the results live for regular use and reference throughout EDF Energy by encouraging managers to make continuing use of their data.

Relaunched in 2008 as the Employee Engagement Survey and working with Towers Watson, the questionnaire focused on three key areas: THINK – people's own role and direction, FEEL – their pride in working for EDF Energy and propensity to recommend, and ACT – their discretionary efforts. The questions were grouped under indices, one being a high-performance index that was used as an element within the bonus structure for managers.

With the integration of the British Energy business the results from the 2009 survey revealed a general thirst for more information about the new vision and how employees could contribute individually and as a team. This led to the development of Our Compelling Story – an interactive workshop to bring that vision alive. This was a huge corporate commitment – it meant taking people away from their day-to-day work for about half a day. These team-based sessions took people through a storyboard of options and exercises to enable them to question and discuss key learning points. Over 96 per cent of employees participated in these sessions over around 10 months. This outcome in presenting an exciting picture with which people could identify and engage was proved in the 2010 survey, which took place roughly half-way through the roll-out of the Our Compelling Story sessions. The feedback showed that employees who had taken part in the sessions responded more favourably, particularly for communications, customer focus, leadership and change management.

Another corporate initiative based on the research feedback related to change management where survey results showed both improvements but also the opportunity to still raise the game. Times of change and transition can cause concern so, to help managers help their teams, the company had a long-standing and award-winning Employee Support Programme. In response to the feedback, a 'Transition Toolkit' was developed and training provided for those leading and managing change. Ensuring the well-being of people was at the heart of this and further developments included stress-awareness communications and training and the launch of 'Less Stress' resources on the Intranet providing pragmatic help and guidance.

With its existing operational fleet and its ambition to build four new nuclear generation plants, EDF Energy probed employee understanding of why it wants to be at the forefront of the new nuclear generation programme in the UK. The results were encouraging but showed more needed to be done especially as the company is keen for its people to feel comfortable discussing these issues with family and friends. The findings led to an ongoing programme of communication with employees to dovetail with externally focused activities about nuclear operations and plans.

'Central to our approach has been presenting information in an even-handed manner,' explained head of engagement and internal communication Ken Hunter. 'It was important for our employees to be given objective information to be able to make up their own minds and have the opportunity to ask questions.'

In developing the communication programme, survey data looked at how different methods of communication worked for different people. An online site was introduced with written and video reports presented by three employees from teams not part of the nuclear business keen to share their own 'nuclear journeys of discovery'. Volunteers from the nuclear business became 'nuclear champions', hosting learning sessions with employees wanting to learn more about the nuclear part of the company. Plenty of time was set aside for asking questions.

Regular coverage of developments and milestones – including those relating to Fukushima – on the Intranet and the company magazine helped build a deeper understanding. All this has also helped to bring together the company following the acquisition of British Energy.

For any survey to be really useful it is vital that its insights are used at a local level as well. This is why EDF Energy made user-friendly materials on departmental results a priority. A particularly successful approach was adopted here by the strategy and corporate affairs function. An Engagement Team was brought together across the function to deliver improvements. Membership rotates every six months with the team taking on specific engagement challenges alongside their normal day-to-day activities. 'Our aim is to increase the number of people who have had closer contact and input to engagement to become beacons of good practice,' explains strategy and corporate affairs programme director Phil Evans.

Key outputs included two flagship workshops for the whole strategy and corporate affairs team to share plans, discuss challenges and work together on solutions. Another about leadership behaviours led to a fresh approach to one-to-one meetings. This involved resetting expectations on the frequency, content and quality of these meetings. Coaching support for leaders was provided and follow-up pulse surveys assessed quality of implementation. 'We've seen an improvement in our leadership feedback scores,' says Phil, 'to amongst the best in the business and comparable with global high-performing companies.'

All these definitions and advice can make it more difficult to define what engagement is for your own particular organization. So when you have decided what engagement means in your organization, where to go from there? A direct question about whether or not the individual feels engaged is too simplistic – and with its varying definitions will not accurately reflect the true position within your organization. Remember your approach to engagement measurement does not always have to be quantitative: group discussions can explore employee relationship with the organization: what strengthens and also what weakens it with specific instances.

An advantage of the quantitative route is the facility to look for the closest links with engagement to prioritize potential action. This will need to be flexible for various groups of staff: by age, level and function. Engagement will mean different things for different people, from the 18-year-old part-timer in retail to the 40-year-old specialist in a profession. So do not make the mistake of assuming one size fits all.

At the risk of adding yet another engagement list, I looked across much of the research into the secrets of engagement and identified eight main themes. This shows that if you spoke to the typical engaged employee you would hear:

- I'm clear about the direction and strategy of my organization.
- I can see what part I can personally play in achieving those aims.
- I'm confident that our senior management is able to lead our business.
- I respect my line manager.
- I'm listened to – ideas, suggestions and criticisms.
- I have opportunities to make best use of my potential.
- I feel that I am treated fairly, am valued and recognized.
- I can trust my organization.

With all the talk of definitions of engagement, we are in danger of forgetting two meanings: first, 'engagement' can also describe a battle or fight. So there can be a negative side: those employees who are bad-mouthing their organizations both outside to family, friends (and anybody else who will listen) and inside to other colleagues. So don't just look at the engaged and what engages them: also examine the disengaged to identify ways they could be turned to a more positive path.

We also need to remember that an engagement usually involves two people making a common commitment prior to a marriage. All the talk of the engaged employee masks the other side of the relationship: What about the role of the other party in this association? Organizations seek engagement from their workforce to improve performance, but do they always reciprocate? So why not have a twin questionnaire for the senior management? When you identify the engagement drivers for your own organization, ask the CEO and senior team to what extent they feel these are given back to their workforce. Comparison with what creates engagement among the workforce and how each is rated with a senior management's viewpoint may provide powerful – and challenging – insights.

Recognition of this mirror aspect of engagement is gaining ground. A Towers Watson global workforce survey found that the most important driver of engagement from an employee perspective was senior management showing a sincere interest in employee well-being. This brings a new perspective to the many definitions of engagement, providing a deeper, wider meaning for the term.

Research by Professor Cary Cooper of Lancaster University Management School and Professor Ivan Robertson of Leeds University Business School showed that a combination of engagement and psychological well-being produces higher levels of productivity than engagement on its own. Co-founders of Robertson Cooper, well-being specialists, they believe that linking employee well-being with engagement is common sense. Ivan Robertson points out that it is difficult to imagine a workforce in which engagement is sustained over a long period but well-being is low: 'If any organization takes a narrow focus,' he says, 'concentrating only on the business benefits of engagement, the key element in engaging employees – management interest in their welfare – is being neglected.' In an article for *Public Servant*, the public service magazine, Ivan Robertson reports that research on employee well-being, particularly psychological well-being, shows a remarkable similarity to research of engagement, making these two perspectives compatible. At Robertson Cooper, based on extensive research in the field, psychological well-being is summarized as employees having:

- a sense of purpose and meaning;
- positive emotions.

When it comes to the enablers and barriers of employee well-being, Robertson Cooper have identified the following six essentials:

- resources and communication;
- control;
- balanced workload;
- job security and change;
- work relationships;
- job conditions.

'Now we need to reap the potential benefits proven by research,' emphasizes Ivan Robertson. He believes that control needs to be devolved from HR departments to line managers to drive local improvements, giving them the tools and support to make engagement fully embedded into working life – not something that is 'done to' employees.

Communication

Internal communication is integral not only to engagement but all aspects of working life. Its measurement usually forms part of annual employee surveys, even if only a few questions. To examine the subject in more depth, specialist communication research can be undertaken. This directs initiatives and investment into the most productive channels. In the past, research tended to focus on the media channels – now we know this alone is not enough.

Think about the three 'M's – the messages carried through the media and their meaning – what it means to employees that could influence or change their behaviour (Figure 8.1).

FIGURE 8.1   The three 'M's

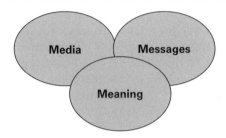

Too much communication research concentrates on detailed questions about communication channels such as publications, not just content and approach but also appearance and even typefaces. Preferred frequency is also asked, even though there is no intention or budget to publish more often. Surely these issues are better addressed by the professional editor with their experience and knowledge?

Evaluation of communication must look more widely – are the messages heard? Understood? Part of working life? Influencing behaviours? To gain an overall perspective of the communication picture in your organization, all these questions should be asked as well as assessment of specific channels or topics.

Publications – either print or electronic – may be the subject: from the company journal to one-off publications. Putting a questionnaire in or with the publication is the easiest option, but it does have a downside. This approach tends to attract a low response rate and those who do answer will – obviously – be those who have opened and at least looked at the publication. So the feedback will be from readers rather than non-readers. Perfectly acceptable, provided you remember that your findings are based on those already interested. However, it will also be helpful to discover why some people do not open or look at the publication – this may be best achieved through focus groups where non-readers can also be included.

After extensive experience in the publication field, Sequel Group managing director Suzanne Peck points out: 'Measuring the effectiveness of your publication is a no-brainer – without it how can you know if what you are doing is having any impact and what else can support your case for investment in our channels?' Suzanne, a long-time supporter of the Institute of Internal Communication, adds, 'We recognize that engaging employees remains a driver for numerous organizations with publications at the heart of the communication, particularly for diverse and hard to reach audiences.'

Relevant questions to assess the impact of your publication might include:

- Is the publication read and if so how much? There will be those who just glance, those who 'graze', picking certain items to read and those who read most of the publication.
- What would persuade people to read more? Content? Approach? Are they gaining sufficient information via other sources?

- A list of attributes, both positive and negative, inviting readers to say which apply: interesting, relevant to me, only gives management viewpoint, simple and direct, often spin rather than substance, open and honest, clear about reasons why decisions are made, often telling me what I know already, helping me feel a real part of my company.

- Many of the above questions could also apply to communication generally. If the publication is about a specific subject (such as benefits) an additional question might be whether it makes clear what the reader needs to do with the information.

Team meetings: research always shows that the preferred means of communication is face-to-face. However, the opportunity offered by team meetings is often unrealized. Indeed, one of the first findings of research in this area frequently reveals that the 'regular' team meetings are anything but regular – and some do not happen at all. You will want to know:

- Do team meetings happen at all? How frequently? How long do they last?

- What is the content? How much organization-wide? How much about the team's own department or function? Are targets discussed with feedback regarding to what extent they have been reached?

- Is there coverage of news that will be relevant to the team such as the latest customer satisfaction scores?

- Do employees have the chance to participate by asking questions, giving feedback and suggestions?

Manager avoidance of holding team meetings may be due to time pressures or little recognition of their value. It may also be down to lack of confidence on holding such meetings, so research results here may lead to training/support for their role. Managers may not realize how much their attitude and body language tells their audience. One manager had to brief her people using information with which she did not agree so just read out the note while sighing heavily and ending with the words 'this is nothing to do with me'. Another manager complained he never had any questions at the end, proving lack of interest in the process. When (privately) his team were asked why, they claimed that he did not really want questions. Why did they think that? 'It was the look in his eyes,' was the response.

Online: so much information is now online in the form of emails and Intranets that it is necessary to ascertain whether this is contributing or detracting from the communication tool kit. Reaction to emails is usually that people feel inundated so it will be useful to discover:

- How many emails fall into the following three information categories: a) essential for my job/great interest; b) helpful for my job/nice to know; c) irrelevant to me/of no interest.

- Asking people to estimate may provide an overview, but this will be based on impressions. A more accurate picture will be provided by asking them to record for one or two days how many emails they received and how they fall into each of the categories above.

- An interesting perspective would also be given by turning the tables from the recipients (who often complain about too many emails) to the senders, asking how many were sent; and how many they consider would fall into these categories. I'm willing to guess that senders see few of their emails as irrelevant but recipients hold an opposite view.

Intranets are an online communication tool that is growing in importance. And with increasingly sophisticated external websites and social media, the organization's Intranet must meet audience needs. For many, the only feedback is the number of visits per page with the assumption being the higher the usage, the better. A leading authority on web communication, Gerry McGovern of Customer Careworks and author of *The Stranger's Long Neck*, a guide to improving online performance, says: 'the number of visits is the worst possible measure of success…'. Gerry asks which has the better experience: the visitor who accesses 20 pages or 10? If 20 pages had to be visited to get the same information as could be obtained in 10, then in this case the fewer visits the better.

This is illustrated by a study undertaken by Interface Engineering into e-commerce websites. Looking at transactions via the website, Gap came top with four times as many e-sales as Macy's. But looking at the number of pages visited per transaction Macy's had 51 per sale transaction while Gap had 12. So an initial reaction that Macy's had more visits and was therefore better would be wrong. In fact, the sought-for information – and sale – was easier at the Gap site. So when undertaking Intranet research, the 'traffic' may give some indication of usage but you may also want to ask if this was because the information needed was difficult to find. You could ask:

- How often do you access the organization Intranet? Give specific times, eg several times a day, several times every two to three days, etc, as options such as 'frequently' may be understood in different ways.

- How easily did you find the information you required? Here you may want to break down various categories from news stories to benefits information.

- Did you find up-to-date information? Or old information (that had not been taken down from the site)?

- Writing style for online is very different from print: questions about length, simplicity, will be particularly relevant here.

Other aspects of Intranet research look at usability and content testing.

'Testing of a company's Intranet website is just as important as testing an external customer-facing site,' says Charlie Barrett, a researcher in web usability. She notes that evaluation for customer-facing websites is increasing, but far less for Intranets, even for these same companies who invest so much in their online presence. In her work she finds the best examples of Intranet sites are as professional as an organization's external website, as easy to use and as relevant to the internal audience as the external site is to its customers.

Usability research supports a user-centred design approach, whereby the end users' needs and requirements are considered at each stage of a website or Intranet's development. Usability sessions are usually one-to-one, involving a moderator sitting with the employee user and asking them to undertake a number of tasks, such as seeking information about a training course, HR procedures or customer service information. These are observed and recorded and outcomes evaluated in terms of various criteria. These might include:

- How easy the tasks were to undertake.
- How long it took to complete or abandon them.
- How logical and seamless it felt to move from page to page.

The richest information is usually obtained with a mixed usability and qualitative approach. This means that as well as evaluating a website or Intranet against practical criteria, it can also be understood in terms of the relevance and appropriateness of aspects such as the language used, overall feel of the site and its fit with the brand. This well-rounded site appraisal can be enhanced with heuristic evaluation that involves rating a website or Intranet against a list of recognized usability principles, which might include:

- The visibility and intuitiveness of 'call to action' buttons such as 'continue' or 'add to basket.'
- The site's use of colour contrast, particularly for visually impaired or dyslexic users.

Events may vary from a training course to a new product launch or Town Hall meeting. People can return from such events having found them 'interesting' or 'enjoyable' but the most effective measurement will be to ascertain what impact the event has had on the audience.

- First, there may be specific basic administration/organization aspects to cover relating to comfort, ease of hearing, etc.
- Did the content cover what the event description promised? In sufficient detail? Relevant to the audience?
- Was there sufficient opportunity to be involved or were they just 'talked at'?
- Depending on the event subject matter and purpose it may also be useful to ask what – if anything – the individual will do differently as a result of attending.
- The initial feedback should be as soon as possible after the event but a follow up, say three months later, will provide additional

insight. By then, those attending will see the event in more perspective and judge to what extent it has helped them or guided their behaviour.

- There may be specific metrics to assess: if the event was about flexible benefits or share ownership, for example, has there been a rise in those participating following the event?

At events, presentations or watching video programmes it is possible to gain immediate feedback from the audience. Hand-held meters for each person enable them to register their responses to specific questions or level of positive reactions to what they hear or see when watching a programme or watching a presentation. For videos, these reactions can be shown on the screen when the programme is run for assessment minute-by-minute. This can be very telling. One video session where employees were able to ask questions as part of the programme, showed that one direct query to the marketing director was met with the long, drawn out response: 'Well ... that depends...'. When viewed later, the positive line on the reaction tracking system dropped sharply at that moment, revealing the answer was seen as avoiding the issue by the audience.

Listening – upward communication

Of course many of these communication channels tend to be one way. The value and importance of listening to people's views within the organization is now increasingly recognized. There are formal methods such as the employee feedback forum, either at meetings or online and more informal ways like managers taking the time to listen to their team. The feedback itself can range from ideas and suggestions to complaints and concerns. Questions here could probe:

- opportunities for feedback generally;
- how well formal methods are working;
- feedback from employees welcomed by senior/line managers;
- feedback from employees listened to/responded to/acted upon;
- confidence in speaking out without recrimination.

Networks – lateral communication

There have always been networks within organizations. Until the advent of social media these were usually local but now diverse people in different roles across countries are able to connect. Such networks can be productive, identifying and sharing best practices and ideas, encouraging collaboration, knowledge management and breaking down organizational silos. However, they can also be negative, distributing bad experiences and gossip as Marc Wright points out in his conversation about social media.

It is, therefore, vital to understand and manage these growing networks. Here are some aspects to look at:

- What networks do people belong to – both internal/external and formal and informal?
- How effective are the formal networks – how could they be improved?
- What information/sharing are specific networks used for?
- Specific examples of productive networking – questions put out/ responded to, problems/issues solved.

Networks often have key people who act as a hub – without compromising confidentiality it may be possible to identify some of these central networkers to make use of their role in creating and managing effective networks. A research approach may be quantitative but this is an area which could repay focus group discussions to probe experiences and identify barriers to overcome and thus stimulate successful networks. It is also possible to gain insights from looking at the various networks themselves and assessing and measuring frequency of usage and typical content.

Change

For employees, change can mean anything from exciting new opportunities to the loss of benefits and even their jobs. In the latter case, research may reveal scepticism and depression and is thus often avoided.

But measurement has a vital role to play as the organization moves forward. Some of the aspects that can help guide communication and HR initiatives through this sometimes difficult period are:

- Direct questions about whether the workforce feels positive or negative about the future: a) for the business; b) for customers; and c) for employees themselves. This can reveal very different reactions. The planned changes can be recognized as good commercially and financially but less positive for customer service. In particular they often doubt if they will be of benefit for the employees themselves.
- Tracking through transition: how do people's views change? In the example in Figure 8.2, wave one was carried out just before a major change to an organization in the financial sector. Then the prime feeling was uncertainty (30 per cent) but six months later this had halved while 'exciting/opportunities' had moved to the top and over a quarter of the workforce were now 'accepting'. Still some way to convince these people that changes will benefit, but the moves from the first to the second research phase showed the organization was going in the right direction, as this chart reveals.

FIGURE 8.2   Tracking through transition

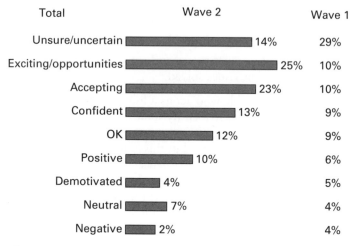

In wave 1 the highest score went to unsure/uncertain but in wave 2 exciting/opportunities leads –

Total	Wave 2	Wave 1
Unsure/uncertain	14%	29%
Exciting/opportunities	25%	10%
Accepting	23%	10%
Confident	13%	9%
OK	12%	9%
Positive	10%	6%
Demotivated	4%	5%
Neutral	7%	4%
Negative	2%	4%

Percentaged on total mentions

- Identifying the change champions and the change cynics. Looking at reactions from those who feel positive about the transition phase and those who feel negative can identify the 'hot spots' – where both the optimists and pessimists are in the company. This is particularly useful when looking at the manager population: if the management strata do not believe in and support the change, they will not be sending the right messages to their team and other colleagues.

- Analysis can also identify the most effective communication in times of change: what works best for those who feel positive about the change process. Typically, employees seek stronger communication and contact with senior management during such times, feeling that those at the top of the organization may have more information about the process and plans.

Remember

- Look for the hot topics within your own organization.
- Think about more than the channel when researching communication.
- Study engagement and choose or develop a definition that is right for your own organization.
- Change can bring opportunities – but it can also cause concern: find ways to discover how people feel; and what could make them reassured and confident.

Emerging issues

09

Other topics are always arising on the corporate agenda so keep your eyes open to see what might be coming up, especially those two aspects of working life rising in the corporate agenda: trust and relationships.

Trust

An essential part of any relationship is trust and this holds true of the relationship between an organization and its people. Trust is becoming higher on management agendas as they recognize its value: it is shown to be linked to turnover intentions, employee well-being and other organizational outcomes in the Kenexa High Performance Institute Work Trends 2011/12 report. The most striking finding from this research is just how important trust is to employees – those who distrust their leaders are about nine times more likely to seriously consider leaving their organization and 15 times more likely to experience stress.

The BlessingWhite Engagement report shows that in Europe and North America only just over half of employees trust their senior management while those that do trust their executives have stronger engagement levels.

India	75%
South East Asia	62%
China	65%
Australia/New Zealand	55%
North America	52%
Europe	51%

This low level of trust in leadership seems to be worsening: in the USA, the Maritz Group found that a quarter of workers have less trust in management than a year ago. The 2012 Edelman Trust Barometer on

Internal Communication and Employee Engagement shows that credibility of CEOs dropped 12 percentage points globally over one year to 38 per cent, its biggest fall since it started 12 years ago. At the same time, credibility of an employee as a company spokesperson jumped from 34 per cent in 2011 to 50 per cent in 2012, stressing the potential role of the employee as an advocate of their organization.

Research into trust can be difficult as it can be hard to define. A topic like this is often best researched through qualitative methods to gain insights into the reasons for lack of trust. A report commissioned from the Cass Business School by the Chartered Institute of Personnel and Development, 'Where Has All The Trust Gone!', looks at the issue of trust, why it matters and what can be done to repair it. When developing questions relating to trust, it would be useful to explore the five types of trust relationships defined by the CIPD with the first two the most important:

- Trust in each other (employees, line managers, senior managers, the organization and its customers, forming a virtuous and reinforcing 'circle of trust').
- Trust in the direct line manager (between employees and their direct bosses).
- Trust in leaders (senior managers, with a tendency to focus on 'heroic' or 'visionary' leaders).
- Trust in the organization (typical of public sector organizations, where individual leaders are less important to employees than the purpose of the organization itself).
- Trust in external relations (such as key external stakeholders, eg customers).

Other questions could relate to the aspects of trust that an International Association of Business Communicators model has defined (see Chapter 10). And if you're looking for one single question a simple 'To what extent do you trust your organization to do what it says it will?' summarizes an overall sense of trust.

Relationships

Trust and relationships were the two key themes emerging from the CEO interviews undertaken by Kevin Murray for his book *The Language of Leaders*. These relationships encompass management and other colleagues. First looking at senior management: their role to clarify the organizational direction and strategy is becoming ever more vital. The evidence of many employee surveys shows that during transitions and change, thirst for communication and contact with the top team, particularly the CEO, grows. But it is precisely at these times that the CEO and senior management are 'too busy' to spend time 'walking the floor' or communicating directly with their people.

The desire to hear directly from the top is frequently down to the perception – often substantiated by experience – that their own line managers do not know the whole story themselves. Survey results showing that employees want to hear more from their senior management team can be dismissed as 'they would say that, wouldn't they'. So it is worthwhile measuring the impact of CEO and senior management relationships and communication.

- Ascertain how people react to a senior management visit: was it a 'royal' tour not interacting with the employees or was it a real visit where they met and related to the workforce?
- If there is a CEO blog or other direct communication from senior managers, look at those who have read it vs those who have not against other characteristics such as understanding and support for the change/direction/initiatives to see if those who have received the communication are more positive.
- Take a baseline before a CEO visit to a location with follow-up a couple of weeks later to measure any change in attitudes.
- Where the CEO has been to some locations and not others look at any differences between those visited and not visited, if any.

That last point is key. Measurement is not always about doing more but could be about less. So if there is no discernible impact from CEO and senior management visits you may want to revisit their approach and format or even halt the programme.

An oft-quoted saying is that people do not leave a company, they leave their line manager. So measurement of those manager strata can provide useful information about what happens in practice and also give feedback to individual managers to help improve their people performance.

Helena Memory of the Hedron consultancy has worked closely with both senior and line manager and points out: 'Like the rest of us, leaders and managers find it easier to focus on the positive rather than the negatives of their personal style and behaviours. I find that helping them identify and play to their strengths is often the most effective route to improve their management performance.'

So looking at the relationships with line managers we need to be asking to what extent are they seen as:

- Competent and 'knowing their job'.
- Accessible when needed.
- Communicating organizational messages clearly.
- Listening to feedback from employees.
- Encouraging and responding to ideas and suggestions.

- Giving constructive performance feedback.
- Showing that they treat their people fairly and as individuals.
- Kept sufficiently in touch by senior management to communicate changes/initiatives.
- Prioritizing customer service.
- A good role model.
- Inspiring.

The results provide crucial information about management style and are specific points that managers can address personally. One young manager had been recently promoted – he was popular with his ex-colleagues but found the transition from work 'chum' to boss difficult. His management style results were dire – the least positive for the whole company. Because he was seen as a potentially valuable manager, the feedback was used positively to support him with advice and training. In the next research phase, he had moved from being one of the worst managers to one of the best. This is not an apocryphal story – I saw it for myself.

Work relationships also include those with colleagues both within and outside immediate teams. Usually within teams relationships are strong – research generally shows that people like the people with whom they work – otherwise they are likely to leave. Results to open-ended questions frequently name work colleagues as one of the best things about working for their organization. However, further afield within that organization, relationships often weaken, leading to silo mentality. Issues that could be explored here include lack of ownership of problems leading to customer complaints being handed ever onwards without resolution, to lack of knowledge and best practice sharing. This could range from general questions about experiences with colleagues to more specific ratings about departments' perceived performance down to knowledge of their work and function.

- Do colleagues treat each other with respect?
- When contacted, how helpful are other departments?
- How well do you understand the role/function of each department (named) within the organization?
- How well informed are you about the other departments?
- Are there opportunities to network outside the team to share best practice and good ideas?

Innovation

Fast arising on the corporate agenda is innovation. Seeking to differentiate themselves from their competitors, organizations recognize that innovation is a key to driving new growth, value for shareholders and competitive advantage in today's global economy. Equally, in the public and not-for-profit sectors, innovation is viewed as vital to bring new solutions to their challenges, service improvements, implementing better processes and cost reductions.

The most obvious way of measuring innovation is the number of new products, enhanced services, cost-cutting actions and, if one exists, the number and practical usefulness of suggestions through an official employee suggestion scheme. But gone are the days when innovation was seen as happening behind the closed doors of the boffins. Ideas, suggestions and original thinking may come from any part of the organization – if the opportunity is there. In terms of assessing the culture and environment to encourage innovation among employees there are some questions to ask both at corporate and line manager level:

- Does the organization encourage new ways of doing things?
- Are ideas and suggestions taken seriously?
- Is there helpful feedback?
- Are 'mistakes' punished?
- Are constructive – even if critical – suggestions welcomed?
- Do people feel they have ownership and control over their work and ideas?
- Does the team share ideas both within the team and other parts of the organization?
- Are good ideas that turn into improvements recognized and celebrated?

Much emphasis is put upon the value of sharing best practice and innovation within organizations. But is this another 'fuzzy' area that is difficult to measure – or even define? Organizations may talk about encouraging innovation but their employees' responses to those questions may tell a different story at grassroots level.

CASE STUDY 7 Can innovation be measured?
Here's how a leading retailer did it

For many years this high street retailer and manufacturer had been associated with high quality and reliability. Market forces and the speed of change meant that those traditional strengths had also become its vulnerability as competitors copied and then overtook them. The organization appointed an innovation director but still the relative stagnation continued. The director decided to explore the reasons in more depth and commissioned a measurement programme that set out to identify how innovation could truly become the lifeblood of the organization.

I was called in to develop a measurement programme that was divided into four phases:

1   Meetings with the CEO and top team to understand the present environment relating to innovation, their aspirations and expectations for innovation.

2   Interviews with managers and professionals in a variety of roles to gain their input and identify the main themes.

3   A quantitative survey to provide hard evidence, identify where the innovation culture could be strengthened and establish a baseline against which to measure progress.

4   An action plan to build on the strengths and address the areas of weakness to move innovation into the organizational culture.

The meetings with the directors soon showed that they claimed to recognize the value of innovation for business success and believed these were rewarded and recognized within their organization. Their description of a vibrant, innovative encouraging atmosphere sounded great – and like many great words it later transpired these were not shared elsewhere or translated into action within the organization. Asked what actions could achieve an innovative culture, they believed these included recruiting and retaining talented people, creating and stretching great teams, recognizing bright ideas and supporting their development.

There was, however, some recognition that these aspirations were not always being met. This became very obvious in the next stage during the discussions with the manager level. From these conversations it became clear there was a disparity between the theory described at senior levels and the reality experienced day-to-day in their working life. They were receiving very mixed messages, which were identified as:

Organizational aspirations They were told:	The day-to-day reality What they saw in practice:
We want to be thought leaders	Safer to let the competition take the risk first
Aim for long-term growth	Work to short-term imperatives
Customers first	Priorities are shareholders and financial image
We must dare to be different	Dependence on safe, traditional brand strengths
Breakthrough in new fields	Past experience comes first

So the messages – theoretical and then in practice – showed that people were being pulled in two completely different directions.

During these conversations I heard two particularly telling stories. In the retail shops somebody had suggested a system whereby the most popular items in the stock room were put at eye level to reduce the stooping and stretching for staff. This was repeated to me several times. However, when I asked who had put this idea forward, nobody knew. A Mr or Ms Anonymous had put forward a great idea – but one that was not recognized or celebrated.

The other emerging issue among the young, ambitious managers was their misleading impression of the organization they were joining. With the supposed emphasis on innovation and invention, the recruitment process focused on enthusiastic professionals bursting with ideas and original thinking. So when the reality of the stagnant conditions hit them, these people were particularly frustrated and demotivated.

The next stage was to look in more depth at these issues through a quantitative phase. Although it was recognized that innovation can come from any level, it was decided in the first instance to research the views of the managers and other professionals where innovation would be seen as an integral part of their role.

A questionnaire was developed to identify ways to overcome the barriers and release the energy and potential enthusiasm for innovation. From the earlier discussions a framework was developed recognizing three key ingredients:

- **Spirit** – the will to innovate evidenced by confidence, exhilaration, energy, adventure and restlessness.

- **Inspiration** – the enthusiasm created among staff to innovate through recognition, trust, challenge, role models, goals and celebration.

- **Structure** – the clear systems to put forward ideas and initiate improvements, teamwork, learning, ownership, communication, performance management and systems alignment with the business.

Questions were developed under each theme so that reporting could reflect these three key areas. First, people were asked directly how their organization could deliver the desired world-class performance. Did they think that it should aim for:

- Keeping its traditional place in their market.

- Developing initiatives slowly but surely.

- Being a fast follower rather than a leader.

- Aspiring to be leading edge, introducing innovations speedily.

Then they were asked to what extent these were achieved in practice. This showed consensus about where they wanted their company to be. In line with the views expressed earlier by the senior management, leading edge was chosen as an aim by eight in 10 but in practice, very few (five per cent) were confident about its achievement.

As 'world-class performer' was a stated objective of the firm, people were asked for their top attributes to achieve this aim: This is what they wanted to see around them in their organization:

- Confidence.

- Recognition of successful staff.

- Learning by experience, including failures.
- Continually seeking to be leading edge.
- Staff being allowed to manage within clearly set and mutually agreed objectives.
- Strategy understood and shared by all.

None of these were viewed currently as strong characteristics. To chart a way ahead, we focused on those most positive about innovation to see what drove those views. Analysis revealed three characteristics. These people were:

- clear about their role;
- could clearly prioritize crucial business issues;
- saw drive and leadership from senior levels.

The research programme had thus clearly identified how people thought becoming a world-class performer could be achieved with focus on three key areas to be addressed to encourage and stimulate innovation and best practice sharing throughout the organization. The gap between senior management's image of innovation and the staff's experience in practice was immense. The most effective action, therefore, was not to simply introduce more suggestion schemes or awards, but for clearer communication and changes to the prevalent culture.

Culture

The culture of an organization or 'the way we do things around here' can be the most difficult area for research to pin down. Focus groups may be the best method here as projective techniques can be used and views probed. However, it is possible to get some quantitative measures.

A list of attributes that may apply to organizational culture can be placed at two ends of a scale, as in the example below, asking where the organization

Teamwork strong	☐ ☐ ☐ ☐ ☐	Teamwork weak
Clients always come first	☐ ☐ ☐ ☐ ☐	Lip service to client service
Listens to employees	☐ ☐ ☐ ☐ ☐	Ignores employees
Open and honest	☐ ☐ ☐ ☐ ☐	Secretive
Addresses poor performance	☐ ☐ ☐ ☐ ☐	Accepts poor performance

is now. So we might find that 30 per cent place their firm in the first two points of teamwork being strong, while 50 per cent choose the two points closest to teamwork weak, revealing that on balance teamwork is seen as inadequate – a point for action.

Probably my favourite question is one that goes to the heart of the culture by looking at an important way it works in practice. This is to ask, who actually 'gets on' in this organization. Who progresses and is promoted? Teamwork, for instance, may be praised – and even highlighted in the organization's values – but is it truly valued? In practice, it may not be the team worker who gets on, but the strong individual loner may be the one who actually progresses and is rewarded. No matter what they are told, employees notice who is given advancement and seen as somebody with potential. So a question gives a list of attributes and asks which describes how people 'get on' here, and then how they should 'get on'. There are often some considerable gaps. Characteristics might include:

- works well in a team;
- toes the line;
- puts quality first;
- knows the 'right' people;
- willing to speak out;
- prioritizes customer service;
- shares good ideas;
- cares for colleagues.

This is the proverbial question that can see senior management claiming 'I didn't get where I am today by…' (when negatives such as 'knowing the right people' or 'toeing the line' come top of the list, as they often do). However, it can be a salutary lesson about how the workforce sees progression to senior levels.

Values

The underpinning of many organizations – and part of the more general culture – are the espoused values. These may have grown up organically over time or more recently defined and communicated. Here measurement can assess the extent to which they are lived in practice. It has been said that the worst way to develop values is for the senior management to go away for an Away Day and return enthusiastically having decided on what the values should be and ready to send these out on posters, mugs, etc. So any accurate assessment of how much organizational values are actually lived by its people can be a reality check for senior management, giving them an important message, and one that can help them turn the dream values from theory into practice.

- What are the values adopted by the organization?
- And to what extent do you see them lived around you? By your colleagues, line managers and senior management.
- Which ways do you see them not lived around you?
- What do you feel the values should be?

This could be done through a questionnaire but may be more productive through group discussions as this lends itself to a more sensitive approach that enables probing initial reactions to get to the heart of the values. An example of this came with one forward-looking organization that decided to test the initial draft of the five values planned for introduction with some focus groups. The word integrity, which was on the list, drew the response from one individual of 'pass me the dictionary'. Another colleague asked a question: she had been told to push an own-brand item which she knew was not as good as the alternative – so would it be showing integrity to do this? Insights like this can help espoused values be turned into real values. The word integrity was replaced with honesty while asking staff to promote items that did not benefit the customer was stopped.

Customer service

In any customer-orientated organization, especially in the retail or public sectors, insight into how employees see customer service compared to the customers themselves is valuable. This may reveal some discrepancies as well as alignment. In one engineering company, staff believed that getting a proposal out as quickly as possible was the top service attribute that potential customers sought. However, from the customer viewpoint, speed was secondary to a well thought out, considered proposal – they were prepared to wait. A simple fact, but an instance of staff responding to the wrong imperative. The customer service/insight team should be able to suggest questions from their research programme relevant for internal use. Some initial ideas:

- How do you rate our customer service? Do you see it as improving or weakening?
- How does this compare to our competitors?
- Do you and the team receive regular feedback about customer service?
- Do you have the opportunity to be involved and suggest improvements?
- What is the best aspect of our customer service? The worst aspect?

In the example in Figure 9.1, from a retailer, customers and staff share similar views – for product knowledge and range, for instance. However, staff underestimated their enthusiasm, which was highly valued by customers, while they considered price as more important than it was in customers' eyes.

FIGURE 9.1   Look for ways to link with key business measures like customer research

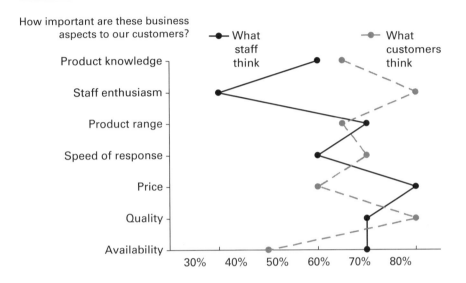

Reputation and brand image

Organizations are increasingly aware that creating and maintaining a positive reputation and brand image is as important internally as it is externally, while it is becoming an ever-growing issue in the public sector. Reputation is about how an organization is seen by its key stakeholders including its employees. It relates to satisfaction, commitment, trust and behaviour, which drive usage and support.

A strong reputation for a strong employer brand both attracts and retains talented employees. As MORI research revealed some years ago, a major influence on public perceptions of an organization is knowing somebody who works there. Therefore the power of the employee to be a positive advocate for your brand is paramount.

There are two aspects to this rating of employer branding and reputation: as an employer and as a business. Reactions to each can differ. In one public sector organization, the staff had great pride in their contribution to society and gave high marks to their organization as a business. However, their employer rating was much lower as it was not seen as a good place to work. Conversely, a financial firm was considered as a great employer, but staff were aware that their commercial offering was not the best on the market, leading to a low business rating.

Brand for Talent by consultant Mark Schumann, emphasizes the need to gain feedback from employees about why they work for the organization – the heart of the brand – rather than imposing what the employer imagines is the motivation. He gives as an example a large dairy conglomerate in the USA which considered their size and coverage was the brand that attracted people to work there. Research revealed that the appeal was quite different. The dairy workers found the product – milk – natural and healthy and this is what they associated with the brand. Another example was a hotel chain seeking to improve its customer satisfaction scores. Again, research among its employees identified four facets of the job of prime importance. The hotel chain responded to these, including language classes in English fluency. Three years later that hotel chain had the highest customer satisfaction scores in the sector.

Experience as a brand manager and later advertising agency CEO showed Simon Barrow, founder of People in Business, that employees often lack the same care, coherence and understanding that a valued customer would expect. His book, *The Employer Brand: Bringing the Best of Brand Management to People at Work* describes the kind of employer brand reputation and experience that will attract and retain the necessary talent, and ensure customer brand promises are widely understood and consistently delivered. To discover more about people's reactions to their brand, here are some areas to explore.

- How do you rate your organization as a place to work and as a business? Its brand image and reputation?
- When asked where you work, what do you say?
- Are you proud/embarrassed to say you work here?
- What attracted you to join this organization? Its products/services?
- Would you recommend this to others as a place to work?

Sustainability and corporate social responsibility

With so much in the news about global warming, depletion of the world's resources and loss of wildlife, ethical considerations such as sustainability and CSR are more to the fore in people's minds. Most employees want to work for organizations that share their values as evidenced by a study by Fresh Marketing in the USA that also identified a strong feeling that important CSR initiatives and information were poorly communicated.

This interest is stronger among the young, especially regarding the relationship with the workforce. Stanford Graduate School of Business found that a reputation for ethical conduct and caring policies towards employees was held to be as important as a job with intellectual challenge and salary level by over 75 per cent of respondents. In the UK, research by MORI identified a link between employer advocacy and CSR with 70 per cent of employees interested in participating in community events.

Organizations recognizing the link between activities such as volunteering are investing more in this area. One example is BUPA where its corporate volunteering programme was expanded after analysing the impact of its initial activities. According to the then BUPA HR director Bob Watson, the initiative created a 'tremendous feel-good factor' throughout the company. This was underlined when the first wave of employee research carried out after the programme saw a seven per cent to eight per cent rise in engagement, a lift Bob Watson ascribed at least in part to the volunteering programme.

So sustainability is coming increasingly to the fore. Leading companies in CSR and sustainability are increasingly looking to ensure their volunteering programmes effectively make use of their employees' core expertise both for the benefit of those employees and the programmes they support. This, combined with imaginative external partnerships, is delivering programmes of real impact. Similarly, these organizations are also asking their employees to innovate product and services that use fewer resources and minimize environmental impact. Robert Nuttall, managing director, corporate responsibility and sustainability at MHP, the communication consultancy, commented, 'The current crop of leading corporates have found that a comprehensive CSR and sustainability programme acts as a huge lever of employee engagement whilst also delivering competitive advantage combined with commercial benefit.'

However, many organizations may claim social responsibility in their corporate literature ('green washing' if not supported by the facts) but fail to communicate to employees or involve them. Research could ask them:

- Awareness of their organization's attempts to reduce environmental impact.
- Understanding of their sustainability and CSR programmes and activities with social or environmental aspects both globally and with the local community.
- Their opportunity to contribute to these activities, and how they might be involved.
- Potential for volunteering via organizational initiatives and any existing outside volunteering activities to identify the current activists.

Mergers and acquisitions

In today's business world an increasing number of organizations are merging, acquiring other companies or being acquired. A huge investment is made and it is estimated 50–70 per cent of such mergers ultimately fail to reach their full potential. In merging organizations, human capital – the talented people they most want to keep – will check out if they are unconvinced and unengaged with the prospects ahead. During this complicated and often difficult time of bringing several sets of employees and their culture together, research is becoming even more important to keep in touch with feelings, identify the most effective ways of providing information clearly and address the challenging process of creating a fresh culture for this new organization.

In addition to covering internal communication – which becomes increasingly more crucial in such times – employee opinion can be sought about:

- Whether people feel they are kept informed as much as possible (taking the financial regulations into account).
- How the merger/acquisition is viewed overall.
- Understanding of the strategic direction.
- Any hopes, concerns and doubts about the change.
- Confidence in the future and the leadership of the new entity.

An interesting perspective was given when two power organizations merged a few years ago, one from the USA and one from the UK. From a list of various culture attributes, employees were asked which described their company as it was then and next which would describe their ideal company and what sort of place they hoped the new organization would be. There was divergence between how people from both companies saw their cultures, with some positives and also negatives.

However, the really interesting angle emerged when the ideal company was described. Despite the differences between current cultures, both groups of employees shared similar hopes for the newly merged organization. This proved to be an encouraging start for uniting two cultures into one.

In our next conversation Jenny Davenport, co-author of *Employee Communication During Mergers and Acquisitions* (with Simon Barrow), shares some of her experiences of merger situations.

Remember

- Trust is a crucial ingredient of a successful business – it can be hard to pin down but needs to be measured and its component parts identified clearly for action.
- One of the most important relationships is with the line manager – questions about management style will provide them with useful feedback.
- A major change causing concern is often when an organization merges with another or is taken over; communication with employees during this period becomes vital.

Conversation 5
Keep in touch with your people during mergers: **Jenny Davenport**, director, People in Business

The last few years have seen an increasing number of organizations merging, acquiring or being acquired, ranging from small firms taken over by larger, to household names joining with other household names. It is estimated that a high proportion of mergers and acquisitions fail while many fail to add value or achieve the anticipated objectives. Research into the reasons behind these failures reveals the prime reason to be lack of attention to culture and people issues.

With her extensive experience of mergers and acquisitions, Jenny agrees with this, pointing out that: 'One of the things the bidder is buying is the expertise, knowledge and reputation of the workforce.'

'It starts with Due Diligence,' she explains, 'I'm surprised that more advisers do not ask to look at the employee research results, which would give them insight into their main asset – their people, particularly those they most wish to retain.' And in cases where no such research exists, Jenny believes this in itself says something about an organization that has not shown an interest in listening to its employees.

The next opportunity for research is during the first crucial 100 days. This is a key period when the experienced, talented people may plan to leave unless they are motivated and confident about the future. There are four main reasons for carrying out some research during this time according to Jenny.

'Firstly, it is an opportunity to get some basic measures in place about attitudes to the employer brand and the most effective communication channels to use during this uncertain period of due diligence.' Then it is also vital to understand what people are feeling at this time; any current fears and rumours – an important insight for management who need to be aware of any issues or problems which might arise.

This can be a stage when people feel powerless to influence events so Jenny believes that research during this period gives them a voice to express their feelings and reactions to the announcement in a safe, anonymous way. Finally – and although this should not be the prime purpose of the research – Jenny points to its role in raising awareness of what is happening, what to expect and to give confidence in the future. It is essential, says Jenny, to be actively listening during this time – a different process than just measuring.

One of the challenges here is the fact that much information needs to be kept confidential while the workforce may be reading speculation in the media. The requirement for confidentiality needs to be communicated quickly and clearly and understanding of this fact can be monitored.

'This is a time when regular measures can give continuing insight and also quick feedback so issues can be addressed,' says Jenny. 'A few questions every couple of weeks can provide a monitor of morale during this period. Look at different populations: analysis by location, department and function can reveal areas where issues may be emerging.'

In her book *Employee Communication During Mergers and Acquisitions*, Jenny suggests five focus areas for internal research.

'A low response rate can indicate a degree of disengagement,' she warns. 'Particularly look for questions relating to credibility and trust – cynicism can undermine the process. Questions about emotional engagement are important as they show how much people want the new organization to succeed.'

This holds especially true for middle managers: 'People will look to these middle manager as change happens – they need to know where the organization is going and its strategy.' Jenny believes that the full value of open comments is often overlooked. She suggests looking at the tone and language as a first-hand indicator of how people feel about the new organization. 'How many are making suggestions and ideas for improvements – this can show how much they care about the business going forward.'

Understanding, interpreting and getting the most from your data

10

Here we look at the ways to make best use of research information and analysis for deeper insights to define a way forward.

As communication manager responsible for the company survey, I was sitting at my desk poring over the pages of computer tables when a colleague remarked 'that looks boring'. He just saw the rows and rows of figures, but I saw something else. 'Not at all, this is the story of our company,' was my reply. Let me confess, I never thought I would find figures fascinating until I received those results.

Since then I find that much of the wealth of the detailed data never receives the attention and interest it deserves – I like to call it a goldmine. Only part of the story is ever discovered. I sometimes wonder why some details – gender, age, etc – are captured when they are often not studied, or understood, in depth.

After the challenges of the questionnaire development and gaining the best possible response rate, comes the excitement of seeing the results for the first time. This is usually in the form of the total overall results – the top line – followed by the detailed breakdown by employee group, age, gender, function, level, location – whatever is specified from the demographic details captured.

However, it is at this point that excitement can fade. You seem to be faced with a mountain of figures too steep to climb. But can I persuade you that this is a goldmine of information and the more you dig the more gold you will find?

FIGURE 10.1 It's a goldmine! Data into information

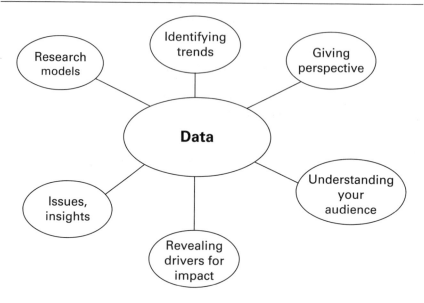

Just one pot of basic data can be used in a whole range of different ways to be turned into management information as shown above. That data is useful for the following:

- Trends and changes over time can be identified where previous research data is available.
- Perspective can be obtained by comparing with other organizations.
- Audiences can be segmented and the views of relevant employee groups understood.
- Analysis can identify key drivers that will show where maximum impact can be revealed.
- Results can be used to contribute towards key issues such as engagement and change.
- Research models can be used to gain deeper insight from the data.

If you are working with an external provider, a report and/or presentation will be given which will provide much of the above information. Nevertheless, do look yourself at the data tables to gain more insights, as you will need to do if you are carrying out your own research.

Before moving on, the first issue to be addressed is the accuracy and reliability of the data – don't assume that if it comes from a computer it must be right. Again, if working with a professional employee research firm this will be done for you, otherwise the task falls to you and it is a vital one. Computers may not make mistakes but a small error in the instructions for analysis can bring mistakes in the data. So it is crucial to check over data to look for possible mistakes or anomalies before moving on to analysis and interpretation. Where scores have been combined on the computer tables, check that the correct bases have been picked up. Are there any typographical errors? Mistakes can ruin research credibility and call all of your work into question. Even one small error makes your audience question how many other mistakes are in the analysis.

And mistakes can happen, even in the most prestigious bodies. One example comes from the early days of the space programme when the Mariner spacecraft veered off course after its launch and had to be destroyed. It was later found that during the data processing phase, one hyphen had been omitted from a code. Arthur C. Clarke described this as the most expensive hyphen in history.

The next check will be calculating the reliability of the data. Before taking the results seriously, people may need to be convinced that the information is robust and reliable. Calculating statistical reliability is covered in Chapter 5 and it is worthwhile making a table showing the confidence intervals for various groups so you can quickly assess which are real differences.

Computer tables typically have the various staff groups across the top of the table with the questions down the side. To make it easier to recognize differences it is useful to combine some scores (eg very and fairly satisfied) and also rank lists in descending order.

It will take some time to familiarize yourself with the computer tables, but it's well worth the effort. Look at them in different ways, not just question by question. Follow through one of the groups – service length for instance. Is there a dip after a couple of years? And after that, do scores consistently decrease or rise again? Where the largest dips occur, that might hint at the reasons for disillusionment. What about the line manager scores? Typically, positivity rises with seniority but what about when there is a sudden drop for line manager level before rising again with senior management? This unexpected finding in one organization going through a major transition was the most significant result of all – the senior management were not taking their direct reports with them on the change journey. Immediate action followed this disturbing insight to introduce business training for the managers to explain the reasons for change.

Trends over time

One of the most valuable aspects of internal research is the ability to compare with a baseline to measure progress over time. So if a survey has been repeated – or indeed, any questions replicated, take a look to ascertain if there are any notable changes. As we have discussed earlier, one or two percentage differences are not significant but, depending on the size of the sample/response rate, you can calculate what a reliable difference is. Changing attitudes and opinions seldom happen overnight unless there is a major organizational change. Experience of many employee research projects has taught me that a negative change can happen quickly – it takes longer for positive improvements to be noticed and longer still to have an impact on workforce opinion.

What sort of changes can you expect to see? Even the optimists cannot hope for a sudden surge – a few percentage improvements over a year is still a good result. Any improvement in double figures is an excellent result. Of course, some findings may plummet due to external factors over which the organization has no control and this should be taken into account.

So when you consider year on year results, do be aware of changes that may impact on your results such as:

- Changes in your departmental structure may mean that the population is considerably different to that surveyed previously. This could result in no difference or a positive or negative one as the employees are not the same people as surveyed before, so any variance may be due to this rather than an alteration in views and attitudes.

- A significant proportion of new starters may increase levels of satisfaction. This is because new employees typically have higher levels of employee satisfaction than established ones and so a department that has recently expanded with many joiners may also see an increase in employee satisfaction, albeit short term.

- When comparing with previous results do look back and consider the organizational context at that time. For example, was the share price performing especially well or badly, was there any expectation of redundancies or had there been a new order secured or any other one-off business activities that could have impacted on employee satisfaction?

- A very different response rate (higher or lower) or a change in methodology might be a factor behind the changes.

If any of these could be responsible, you may wish to take them into account but not make them an excuse. It is not possible to 'calculate' the strength of that influence. Managers sometimes ask if there is a figure that can be added or subtracted to compensate for certain circumstances. The answer is no, this is a snapshot in time so reasons may explain changes but there is no magic number to factor in.

Perspective

Benchmarking against other organizations has its pluses and minuses. On one hand this provides useful perspective to an organization's own results, but be warned, it can take over to the detriment of the project. Two examples. At one presentation, the senior team became so interested in where they measured up, that they clearly ceased listening to the important messages.

After every point they called out 'how do we compare against the norm?' The competitive spirit had taken hold. In another company, senior managers were told that only a quarter of their people had confidence in their leadership. Gloomy faces. But when they heard this was, in fact, marginally better than the national average, smiles all round. But, although not as poor as elsewhere, this was a dire reflection of the leadership.

Used thoughtfully, benchmarking adds value and insight to the findings. This particularly applies to perspective by different countries. Here differences in culture and environment have an influence on country results that are important to understand. The chart below shows the engagement levels by country from the engagement surveys conducted by Towers Watson among four million employees in about 400 multinational companies. If the scores seem high, remember that these are multinationals that take sufficient interest in their people to research their engagement but they are a subset of the total workforce – national workforce levels are lower but show the same highs and lows within countries.

Japan	66	Slovakia	83	Egypt	86
France	73	Australia	84	Greece	86
Luxembourg	73	Canada	84	Saudi Arabia	86
Finland	74	Hungary	84	South Africa	86
South Korea	74	Ireland	84	Taiwan	86
Hong Kong	76	Israel	84	Ukraine	86
Italy	78	Malaysia	84	Brazil	87
Spain	78	Morocco	84	Indonesia	87
Belgium	79	Norway	84	United Arab	
Germany	80	Sweden	84	Emirates	87
United Kingdom	80	Switzerland	84	Vietnam	88
China	81	Thailand	84	Kazakhstan	89
Netherlands	81	Bulgaria	85	India	90
Czech Republic	82	Portugal	85	Mexico	90
Singapore	82	Romania	85	Philippines	90
Slovenia	82	Tunisia	85	Venezuela	91
Austria	83	Turkey	85	Columbia	92
Denmark	83	United States	85		
Russia	83	Chile	86		

Most major employee research providers have extensive normative databases with specific sets of questions to allow for comparison. Many are useful to gain perspective, but ensure that you do not use these wholesale, it is also essential to have your own, individual questions. Most benchmarks are only available to those employing that particular research agency. However, one employee engagement research agency, ORC International, does offer free benchmarking reports to organizations that attend their benchmarking group meetings and submit data from their survey to be included in the database. That database, *perspectives*, holds data from more than 400 organizations, representing the views of 1.4 million employees worldwide, ranging from central government to retail.

Be wary of producing too many comparisons. It can hide the real impact of the results. Also remember that employees are not stupid, so avoid trawling to find poor performers to compare against in the hope of looking good. If you look long enough you can always find companies with worse results, but this would defeat the object of the exercise.

Understanding your audience

When first received, the overall results seem fascinating. But questions soon emerge: what do managers feel? Are the results very different by department? Location? What difference does service length make? Are the younger people more/less positive? It is often in this information that much of the value lies and the identification of specific potential action points.

However, when contrasting department or location results you will need to put these into perspective. People in a fast-moving marketing department are likely to be very different from those in accounts, so comparing their results against each other may not be useful unless the results reveal deep-seated problems that go beyond job-type differences.

Location too can be a major factor. In some towns there is only one major employer while in others there is more choice. Employees in large cities tended to seem more negative and demanding than colleagues elsewhere as they had a wider selection of potential employers. That was before the recession, so that difference may not be so marked now.

CASE STUDY 8   The Civil Service in the UK: joining together in a single voice

A powerful voice for Civil Service people is provided by the UK's largest staff attitude survey covering attitudes and experiences of work. Until its launch in 2009, staff surveys were conducted separately by Civil Service departments and agencies in different parts of the UK. Individually, they had been useful in terms of tracking progress on priority areas and identifying potential action. However, these separate surveys lacked one single voice – they were inconsistent, carried out at varying times with different questions, wording, scales and reporting structures making meaningful comparisons between organizations difficult.

There was a strong need to get a clear picture across the whole organization to focus resources and expertise into improving front-line public services, plus the nationwide pressure on reviewing costs, which suggested that an annual standardized Civil Service-wide survey would be more efficient and effective. In 2009 a small pilot study was undertaken in nine departments and agencies to develop and fine-tune the questionnaire and the research process. It was managed by the Cabinet Office Civil Service Capability Group working closely with the departments and in consultation with the Council of Civil Service Unions. Reassurances were provided that appropriate standards would be met for data protection, privacy and identification of individuals.

This harmonization process brought some challenges that needed to be resolved as Matt Kerlogue, head of Employee Research Analysis and Insight at the Cabinet Office, explains:

> One issue was the need to preserve useful tracking questions which had measured progress over some years. The need for convergence had to be balanced with a questionnaire that met the needs of the participating departments. We matched questions where possible and developed a core questionnaire which also had flexibility for local questions specific to each organization for topics not covered in the core.

When that survey was launched in October 2009, this was the first time all government departments asked the same questions of all their staff to give Civil Service leaders a clear picture of their entire organization. At that time, director of human resources at the Department of Transport, Mervyn Thomas, said: 'The best employers now recognize how crucial employee engagement is in enabling their staff to fulfill their full potential, so I'm delighted that the Civil Service is undertaking Britain's largest-ever engagement survey.'

Since then the survey – carried out in 96 government organizations and open to nearly half a million Civil Servants in 2011 – has given consistent measures of employee engagement and staff attitudes with a good median response rate across the participating organizations of about 77 per cent. A benchmark Civil Service engagement index and reports with individual results are produced for over 8,000 management units.

With this wealth of information, it was recognized that a process needed to be put in place to ensure it was used productively. A network of engagement practitioners from each of the participating organizations was set up to share knowledge and best practice and take a lead role in turning those results into tangible improvements. They act as a virtual team and provide feedback to the central Employee Engagement team.

The importance of understanding and interpreting the results was also recognized. Advice on interpretation emphasized that staff surveys should not be looked at in isolation but need to be set into context against other measures, such as delivery against business plan objectives, workforce data, and external assessments such as Investors in People to gain a rounded picture of performance.

An advantage of the combined approach is the efficiency of a single procurement exercise that has delivered strong value for money; the 2011 survey cost just 38 per cent of the total that individual departments and agencies had spent on staff surveys in 2008/09 before the single survey was set up. 'We are continually learning and improving the process,' says Matt. 'It has become faster and more efficient – with an automated process we can get Business Unit results out within four weeks.' Looking ahead, he believes there could be opportunities with attitudinal segmentation to add value to the process.

However, a standardized approach can hide key differences among a disparate workforce that includes policy advisers, job centre workers, prison officers and coastguards, while an annual survey may not always be able to keep up with a fast-changing business environment. Therefore some parts of the Civil Service carry out supplementary research on a more regular basis.

At BIS (the department for Business Innovation and Skills) director of communication Russell Grossman introduced a monthly Pulse survey. This tracks 19 questions from the main survey focusing on leadership, managing change, engagement, work and organizational purpose. This is valuable in keeping in touch throughout the year, says Russell: 'We ensure that the same people are not surveyed each time, we ask a different 100 out of our 3,000 workforce and keep up a consistent 60 per cent response rate.'

Russell notes that one of the most powerful feedback for senior management lies in the qualitative verbatim comments of BIS people. 'What they say, reflects real life in our business,' he points out, 'and as such has a real impact – sometimes more than just the figures themselves because senior management can listen directly to the experiences and suggestions of the staff here.'

Finding the keys

The mountain of information may become daunting: out of all that feedback, what is most important? Where will attention and action have the biggest impact? There is a type of analysis that can help identify the places for you to focus on. Known as key driver analysis, this takes one question (eg communication, trust, etc) and looks at the closest links with the positive reactions across all the other questions in your survey.

Thus it can identify which have the strongest link with those who rate communication as good or who have high trust in their organization. Those with the most impact are called 'key drivers', which will highlight the priorities among all that information.

This type of technical statistical analysis is usually carried out by a statistician. However, a simpler approach is possible if just basic information is required. To do this, in addition to the demographic groups being analysed in the computer tables, a further attitudinal analysis based on two points of view can be added, for instance:

1 Those who find communication good.
2 Those who find communication poor.

The results from these two groups can then be examined across all the other questions to ascertain the views of those rating communication highly and those rating it poorly. This reveals any telling differences between the two groups. The largest divergences will show the areas of greatest impact for good communication. This is illustrated in the table opposite, which takes the two groups – 1) communication good; and 2) communication poor – across those who also gave good marks for questions about training, team meetings, the Intranet and CEO Blog.

TABLE 10.1   Percentages finding communication good or poor

	55% find communication good	45% find communication poor	Difference
Training good	52%	48%	4%
Team meetings good	70%	30%	40%
Intranet good	55%	45%	10%
CEO blog good	65%	35%	30%

So looking at the above results, we conclude that there is little link between people finding communication good and also training (only four per cent difference) and slightly more for the Intranet (10 per cent difference). On the other hand, there is a strong link between positive reactions to the CEO blog and positive feelings about communication (30 per cent difference) and an even stronger link with team meetings (40 per cent). From the research purist view, we must remember that we are looking here at correlations and links – not cause and effect. However, it does indicate here that good communication is connected with CEO blog and team meetings.

That is, however, only one half of the story. How is performance against these strongest links with communication or whatever aspect you want to investigate in more depth? If the strongest correlation is team meetings and the findings show they get high marks then all is fine. If, however, team meetings are poorly rated then they will be a priority for action. The chart below illustrates this.

FIGURE 10.2   Identifying priority areas to improve internal communications

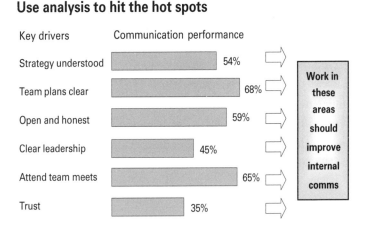

Here, we look at two aspects to gain deeper insights. First, the strongest correlations between good communication ratings and other survey questions to identify which have the greatest impact on positive feelings about communication (key drivers on the left in order of strength). Second, how each scores to prioritise where action will have most impact (the bar charts). Here the top driver of good communication – strategy understanding – scores 54 per cent: trust and leadership are also relatively poor performers. Focus on these key areas will have the maximum impact to improve communication.

Issues insights

Another way to dig in that goldmine is to look at the issues that may have sparked the research in the first place to bring them to the surface. So here you would be looking through the results by relevant issue to examine reactions by employee profile (age, level and so on). Other, unexpected, issues may appear too. Don't close your mind to these – if something strikes you as unusual or strange, try to follow this through to understand in more depth.

Research models

Make best use of various models already developed and researched that can be used as a working hypothesis. These models will have been developed by individuals or organizations either as a hypothesis based on their observations/ experience or regression analysis to identify statistical links. The aim is to understand the crucial dimensions of a specific aspect to measure and then target improvements on that aspect.

One model created via statistical analysis looks in depth at trust – developed as a project for IABC (International Association of Business Communicators, see Figure 10.3). Organizational trust is increasing in importance at the same time as it is being eroded both in business and public life. This trust model starts by showing the relationships of trust to job satisfaction and to perceived organizational effectiveness.

Next it moved on to reveal five main ingredients that can strengthen – or weaken – employee trust in their organization.

So what can we learn from this model? It shows that trust is linked to:

- **Competence:** how competent is the organization and its leaders?
- **Openness/honesty:** is information delivered in a transparent way?
- **Concern:** does the organization demonstrate sincerity, caring and empathy with its people?

FIGURE 10.3 Drivers of trust

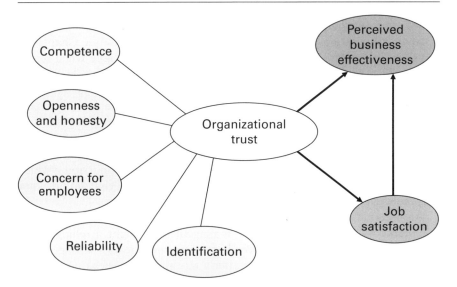

(International Association of Business
Communicators trust model)

- **Identification:** is there a common ground of shared goals, values and beliefs?
- **Reliability:** does the organization show consistent and dependable actions?

It may be that your research already contains questions that cover these concepts. If not, you may wish to use these themes and add questions under each main heading. To gain an overall score for each trust driver, for simplicity, an average of the positive scores can be a useful indicator. Looking to build trust, this will make it clear which aspects are getting low scores and are potential for improvement.

There are many other models in the market such as the Gallup 12, which Gallup describes as a series of simple workplace questions that can spark employee–management action with measurable results. One of these, having a best friend at work, is sometimes felt to be less relevant in different cultures.

Other models are continually being developed to explain business issues such as communication and engagement – if you look on the web you will find a host of such models. There is a school of thought that finds such templates limiting and sometimes actively misleading so you will need to take a close look and make use of those which most closely match the needs of your organization.

What they say ...

By focusing on what the data has to tell you, don't forget the responses to the open-ended questions. These need to be coded into themes (see Chapter 6) but the words themselves bring the research to life, especially when senior management realize this is the authentic voice of the workforce. Sometimes this has more impact than the figures. When reporting back to one retail firm that staff found the workload too heavy, there were smiles around the board table. 'They always say that,' was the response. The verbatim quote was read out describing a long queue in one branch and a ringing phone that was answered by a despairing customer as staff did not have time. This silenced the laughter. It became a finding that was taken seriously for action – which proved successful from the subsequent follow-up survey that found work was more evenly distributed.

An international focus group project about the encouragement and acceptance of upward feedback by management brought a telling quote from Brazil: 'The dog which has been bitten by a snake fears a sausage.' That really summarized the sense of fear after a reprimand for speaking out.

A word of warning here. Be careful that your selection of verbatim comments reflects a body of opinion. The day following one presentation a call was received from the MD's secretary. I was thrilled – the interest must be great for such a quick follow up. But the question was quite specific: 'Re the quote about the fact the MD had a foreign car, how many had said that?' In fact it was only one person – the MD was relieved but his obsession with that one observation had obscured the major messages of the whole project.

Thoughtful consideration of the data to turn it into management information is time consuming. Why not get some colleagues to help? Perhaps some management trainees or a survey project team could take this on as a project with each individual or small team given one particular aspect (eg differences by gender) to study in depth before reporting back. Not only does this save time but it also gives greater ownership of the measurement throughout the organization.

A goldmine needs deep excavating so one consequence of a detailed examination of the data can be the wish for further analysis. Do not get caught in the analysis paralysis trap. It is tempting to ask for more and more cuts of the data – after all, that puts off the fateful day of identifying specific action points to address.

Take a balanced view. In some instances additional analysis will help clarify the picture and provide extra insights. Overall gender analysis, for instance, can hide important information. On the surface, views may seem to be the same. With the glass ceiling in mind, is there a difference between men/women's views at manager level? So you may want analysis by level as well as gender. Looking at the important line manager cadre, does age make a difference? Younger managers may have quite different views to their older colleagues.

When you are ready to move on to the next phase, do not just lock the data tables in a drawer. They contain information that could be useful in the future. On-the-ball communicators and HR people keep them as a reference so that if issues arise or initiatives are contemplated there may be relevant information therein. Do not put up a closed sign outside that valuable data goldmine.

Interpretation

When you have wrung all the information you can from the data, take a step back. Now is the time to take a pause on the research journey. The organizational story is in there – you need to discover and interpret that hidden narrative before sharing it with the feedback and planning phase. Sometimes 'thinking time' is dismissed as wasting time. However, many potentially valuable insights can be lost through too much haste. Look across all the data to put the information in perspective, find common themes, mysteries that may need closer examination. Make use of the types of analysis described above for deeper understanding. Think about external factors, the employee profile, potential challenges and opportunities for the business and how these might be woven into the story. The research results are part of – not separate from – the organization and need to be integrated into the bigger picture of business planning. Look for the areas of weakness to address but do not forget to recognize the equally vital strengths on which to build.

Remember

- Start by studying the raw data in depth to see what valuable management information it is showing.
- Get more analysis where it assists understanding of an issue or employee group.
- Keep the data to hand – the information it contains can continue to inform the business in the future.
- Take the time to interpret and understand the data before moving to the next stage of your research journey, turning it into constructive information.

Turning the results into the organizational story

11

This chapter describes how to develop that information into interesting and thought-provoking feedback focusing on the all-important first presentation to senior management.

'I have made this letter longer than usual, only because I have not had the time to make it shorter,' said Pascal. How true this is of presentations. Death by PowerPoint describes how many research results are presented. This presentation software has its advantages – easier to use and faster than previous lecture methods. However, the very ease of producing charts and text has also brought its dangers.

The US military took a stand against PowerPoint some years ago. One extremely complex slide was nicknamed the 'bowl of spaghetti' while one commander said that when they understood the slide, they would have won the war and another added 'it's dangerous because it can create the illusion of understanding.'

Before a fuller presentation, consider a one-page summary to get the main points across. Senior managers often ask for summarized one-pagers highlighting the main points rather than long time-consuming reports. You will have a wealth of material so producing a succinct story may be a challenge. It might look like the summary below.

ABC plc 2012 survey summary

The response rate (80 per cent) and the fact that the Engagement Index (EI) score continues to rise show that the ABC workforce are becoming more confident despite the continuing changes and uncertainty. The latest EI score seems low but is above the industry average, while the level of participation is high for the sector.

Engagement Index

2012: 60%
2010: 51%
2008: 47%
2005: 43%

Business

People are strong champions of the business with just over three-quarters speaking highly of ABC products and services. Confidence in the way the directors are leading ABC shows a significant improvement – now marginally more are confident (plus three per cent). However, customer service will need to be investigated: although six in ten have sufficient opportunity to provide service this has fallen eight points.

Communication

Against the perception of poor communication typically found in times of change, the ABC score for level of information has risen to 60 per cent – a three-point rise suggesting that action following the previous survey is meeting with success. Upward communication has a slight reduction of four percentage points, a somewhat disappointing result although still better than other change companies.

Employer

Rating as a place to work sees a small decrease that is due to issues related to skills and abilities, which remain a concern to staff. Although more development is wanted, it is encouraging that seven in ten have a feeling of worthwhile work accomplishment.

Action

Looking at improvements, people suggested that better efficiency, streamlined processes and preventing waste would help ABC become more financially successful, in line with the 45 per cent saying departmental communication could be better.

This type of early 'heads up' can stimulate interest in more depth. When giving feedback, particularly to senior management, just showing masses of charts is the easy option. The fact that many data packages can also generate graphs and tables is a mixed blessing – useful to look at the data initially, but to turn that information into a coherent, insightful story you need thoughtful consideration, imagination and, above all, time.

An earlier chapter described how to get the best from your data to turn it into management information. When it comes to giving life to that information, there are three main steps:

- **Content**: the main themes and story.
- **Approach**: how to tell that story and its visual effect.
- **Surprise**: unusual ways to get the story over.

It can be disconcerting to present to a group of senior managers, especially if there is some bad news to impart. If you are working with a professional agency as independent outside advisers, then it is sometimes easier for *them* to communicate those difficult messages. As an internal staff member it may be harder. Take confidence, as the facts speak for themselves, and word your comments to make it clear this is the voice of the workforce, not your personal opinion. Get to know the data in depth so you are not surprised and undermined by a query you are unable to answer.

Focus on one aspect that might be keeping the CEO and senior managers awake at night, as the saying goes. In this example, this public sector organization was going through a major change. Concern that the leaders may not be taking the workforce with them was a crucial issue. So we selected specific questions that reflected employee understanding, commitment and involvement with the changes and analysed those who agreed with all (the convinced), those who disagreed (still in the past) and the undecided (the fence sitters). This thinking was based on the transition model in William Bridges' book, which divided people into the three categories: at the beginning, at the ending and in what he describes as the 'neutral zone'.

Our analysis revealed that over six in ten were in the positive category: at the beginning. So we decided to raise the bar and look at those who felt strongly – here we found one in five, whom we named 'change champions', as likely to be the enthusiastic and energetic ones to drive change forward. At the end of the presentation the CEO said that this one chart told him the essential story of his organization (Figure 11.1).

FIGURE 11.1   Sometimes one chart tells the story ...

Where your people are on the change journey...

(Based on William Bridges' transition model)

This was, of course, at top level. Boring down into departments and levels revealed different pictures to focus action. We also analysed the change champions' characteristics to identify what communication and HR aspects were most closely linked with their positive attitudes. Figure 11.1 tracked progress at the BBC some years ago as case study 9 shows.

The Refuseniks – be aware there may well be some in the senior management team who refuse to accept the results. They may look for all kinds of excuses and some even suggest there is 'something wrong' with the data, I have even been asked if the computer might have mistakenly reversed the results, so sure was that manager that the results would be more positive. These refuseniks are becoming fewer as the top team and managers become more realistic, especially during recent difficult times – but be prepared.

Content

Return back to the original thinking and reasoning for this project. If you took the advice in Chapter 1 you will have an outline aspirational presentation to hand. Some findings may influence that original approach but it will make a good start. Do take your time – search for the main messages emerging. As discussed earlier, the data is a goldmine of information but this is not the time to go into great detail that may obscure those important overarching messages. Take it step by step:

- From all that information, look for the five or six crucial ideas that you want to impart. These may be organization-wide issues or relate to specific groups such as managers or customer-facing staff. Don't be tempted to try and cover everything. If you are concerned that the senior management team will feel there is relatively little output for considerable input, explain that these are the headline findings and there is a mass of information to support the conclusions. I was once advised to come with only six to eight slides to present to the board. To achieve this took more time, but it worked – at the end, the director making the suggestion said his point had been proved – it was possible to communicate the results succinctly and simply without losing important information.

- Remember that it is as vital to build on the strengths as it is the weaknesses. So if strategy is misunderstood but the line manager relationship is firm, this suggests an avenue to impart that information. Very few organizations have no good news to report at all – so balance any presentation by acknowledging the strong points.

- To align with what is important to the business, return to the main themes to report back under these headings. This is the way one organization did it. From the start there were four key areas to explore and results were grouped under these themes, agreed to be an integral part of success for that business. To create one summary figure for each, an index was developed with questions grouped under four main headings and an average calculated based on the positive scores to each as shown below:

- **Choice**: employer of choice: attracting and retaining talent questions.
- **Commercial**: business success and customer service questions.
- **Clarity**: clear leadership and common purpose questions.
- **Culture**: what it is like to work here questions.

This was a quick way to see the relative position of each, backed up with the results for each question under its heading to provide more detailed feedback. Each department, function and level was subsequently given their feedback in this way so the whole survey process was both direct and consistent.

Before you move on to putting the presentation together, check how long is provided on the agenda. Board presentations have been known to allocate just 15 minutes while others are willing to spend an hour plus. Make sure that you keep to this timing and allow space for questions and comments. If you engage your audience, they may have queries or want more details about a specific aspect to follow up at a later stage.

Approach

'Tell them what you're going to say, say it, and then tell them what you said.' Start the presentation with an upfront summary of the key messages you will cover before moving on to the evidence that supports those findings, which should be summarized again in the conclusions. In terms of approach:

- Take a look at how information is presented regularly to the senior management: financial updates, customer research, etc. For some organizations, the most effective way to present internal research will be to replicate a similar format so the senior team see these in the same business terms as other management information.

- If there is a Dashboard or Balanced Business Scorecard, then put the internal survey up there as part of the key indicators of the business.

- Ensure there is a logical flow and the information is clear so your audience does not have to work too hard to understand.

- Don't just repeat what is on the screen – your audience will find it hard to read and also listen at the same time. They can see the information for themselves – give them time to read and then draw conclusions and summarize what the information means. It is a good time to add in a few direct quotes from the verbatim comments to support the figures.

- To recommend or not to recommend – that is the question. A fully fledged action plan cannot be expected at this stage, but attention on the areas that call for action should be included. This might comprise a list of questions such as: 'How are we going to build on the great relationships most line managers have with their team?', 'Why are team briefings not happening regularly?', 'Where are the issues making our people believe that customer service could be better?'.

- In terms of visuals, much depends on the culture of the organization. If the senior managers are accustomed to charts and figures you may want to keep to that format. Otherwise the information can be communicated in other ways. Below are two examples of how organizational advocacy could be illustrated.

FIGURE 11.2   Look for original ways to present your data

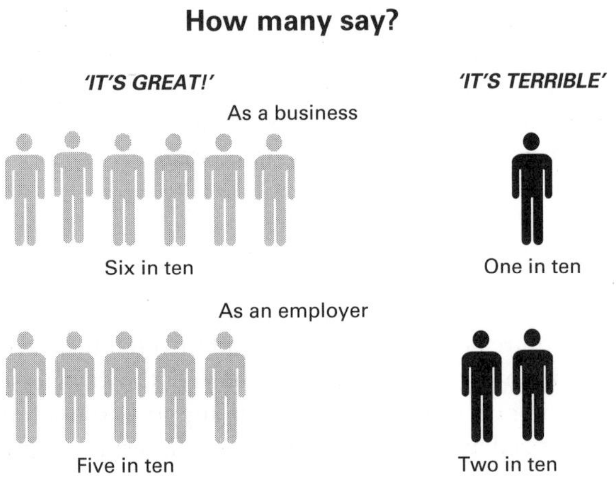

How many say?

'IT'S GREAT!'   **'IT'S TERRIBLE'**

As a business

Six in ten   One in ten

As an employer

Five in ten   Two in ten

FIGURE 11.3   Graphic illustration of the concept of organizational advocacy

What makes a champion?

I feel involved and able to contribute

I believe in my organization

I'm proud to say I work here

I'm aware of what's going on, give feedback – and they want to listen!

If you are interested in knowing more about original, inventive ways to present data, David McCandless, a London-based author, writer and designer, has written a great book, *Information is Beautiful*, or check out his website. He says his passion is visualizing information – facts, data, ideas, subjects, issues, statistics, questions – all with the minimum of words. 'My pet-hate is pie charts,' he says, 'Love pie. Hate pie-charts.'

Think about how you might be able to segment employees to focus minds on specific issues to give an overall organizational picture. Take two questions, in our example about communication: upward and downward. By cross-analysing one question by the other five, groups will be identified (Figure 11.4). Those who felt:

1 Informed by their organization and able to make their views known: the '**connected**'.

2 Informed by their organization but unable to make their views known: the '**silent listeners**'.

3 Not informed by their organization but ready to make their views known: the '**outspoken uninformed**'.

4 Not informed by their organization and unable to make their views known: the '**disconnected**'.

5 That they did not have firm feelings either way: the '**fence sitters**'.

More depth can be given by learning more about these five groups: where are most connected people found? The disconnected? Further insight can look at what communication channels are most used by the 'connected' so these can be strengthened for the others.

FIGURE 11.4   Communication profile

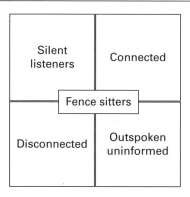

Think about how you might segment the workforce – the talented people who the organization wants to retain, the traditional worker on whom the organization depends – and the transients – those who are passing through.

Each has two sides – they could be 'stars' or 'black holes' – bring this to life by quoting what they might be saying ….

FIGURE 11.5   Bringing segmented data to life

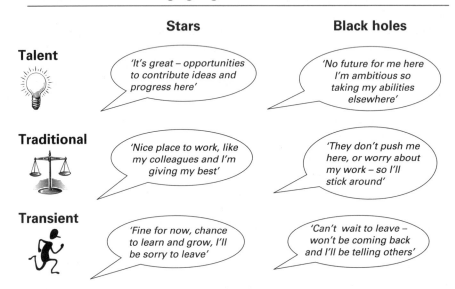

These are just a few examples. Look at your data and think of other analysis that will give deeper understanding, especially in relation to business or public value issues. For instance, those who understand the strategy could be analysed together with those who can see they have a part to play in fulfilling that strategy, which would give a combined figure of the strategy activists. There are many fascinating insights if you look for them.

Surprise

Some of the results may be a surprise in themselves but senior management have been known to shrug off results with the comment: 'I knew all that already.' One way of avoiding this is to follow the advice Sir Robert Worcester gave me when I first joined MORI. He counselled me to ask senior management to complete a prediction questionnaire prior to the presentation so their forecasts could be compared to the actual results otherwise they will claim the findings coincide with their expectations. On one occasion I forgot and sure enough, at the end of the presentation the CEO said dismissively: 'Well, no surprises there.' A prediction questionnaire can avoid this reaction – and it is surprising in itself that some senior management guesses are either wildly over optimistic or even pessimistic.

XXX survey prediction questionnaire

This prediction questionnaire asks you to estimate some of the responses to the XXX staff survey. Plus what you would ideally – but realistically – wish to see as the target score. The individual responses will remain anonymous and only an average of all the scores will be shown.

What percentage do you think/would you ideally like to agree with the following?

	Target	Prediction
XXX is a great/good employer	…%	…%
XXX is a great/good business	…%	…%
I feel proud to work for XXX	…%	…%
The changes relating to Project A were well handled	…%	…%
I rate XXX's service to clients as excellent/very good	…%	…%
The XXX board has a clear vision of where the company is going	…%	…%
I feel well informed about what is happening in XXX	…%	…%

When it comes to surprising presentations you will need to be careful. In a fast-moving lively company I once dressed as a doctor, complete with white coat and stethoscope, dividing the results into 'good health', 'slight temperature' and 'medicine needed'. That went down well but next day's presentation was to a law firm; as you can imagine, the same approach would not have been appreciated. So a more creative approach to a presentation needs to be handled carefully – think hard about the organization culture.

CASE STUDY 9 BBC: meeting the needs of a challenging audience

Looking forward to directing and planning communication and human resource efforts is a main focus for research. However, it is often valuable to look backwards to track progress over time, especially when this reveals that action undertaken has been effective.

This was the case at the BBC some years ago for the internal communication team led by Russell Grossman. Their goal was to improve communications with perhaps the world's most demanding audience – creative, challenging, busy professionals, which included journalists, presenters, technicians and digital experts – all with particularly high expectations as they worked for the internationally respected British public service broadcaster. At that time, response rates for the staff research were low – usually below 30 per cent, which reflected both the work pressures and low expectations of any action stemming from the survey.

Although the regular staff survey included a few questions about communication, a separate research project was undertaken to examine this in greater depth with specific questions exploring the channels, team briefing and upward communication opportunities. A new focus ensured that the results were fed back to managers while the internal communication team took on board the results when making their plans for the year ahead.

As expected, there were some criticisms of communication but what was particularly encouraging was that any action would be on a positive base – over nine in ten of BBC people were actively committed to help the BBC succeed and were strong advocates of its programmes, services and products.

One emerging issue was the declining interest in the internal newspaper, *Ariel*. In view of the major investment in this weekly publication it was important to understand the reasons for the fall-off in readership. The project took three phases. The first was a series of focus groups with BBC staff in different roles and regions. The main message here was that the BBC sought objectivity in its external reporting and staff wanted to see the same objectivity for their internal journal. However, they were realistic in their expectations, appreciating that *Ariel* was available outside the BBC and open to press coverage.

It was clear that a balance was sought and in the next phase of group discussions two optional redesigns were trialled as well as looking in more depth at what readers really wanted. They were asked to put themselves in the editor's shoes and draft a front page containing the top news they expected to see. This provided much useful input for changes and feedback from the final series of focus groups, discussing the new version, showed that those changes had increased the readership. Since then there has been a further development with *Ariel* keeping up-to-date by going digital recently, a move that has proved successful.

Although many of the initiatives came from the internal communication central team, they also recognized that much action needed to be taken at local level. A system was put in place to get the results back to the departments both at the centre and in the regions with a team trained to present the results and help develop action plans.

This approach soon showed results in terms of encouraging staff to participate, with the response rate gradually increasing as they saw action following their input. By 2010 the response rate had risen to its highest ever of 65 per cent. Major improvements were also seen in the communication quality index started back in 1996 to track progress over time (Figure 11.6). This comprised an index of eight key core questions repeated in the surveys over six years. These included level of information, its consistency, credibility, timeliness, clarity, conciseness, openness and honesty – all aspects viewed as crucial to BBC people's perceptions of their communications.

FIGURE 11.6   The BBC's communication quality index improved over time

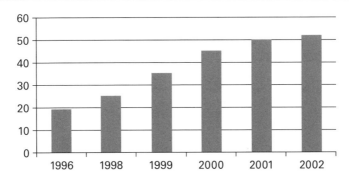

The chart shows the success of the communication efforts rising from just 19 per cent in 1996 up to 52 per cent six years later. This showed the value of identifying specific core questions that could be retained consistently to measure change over time as well as having the flexibility to introduce new aspects to keep the questionnaire up-to-date.

As internal communication gradually became a core part of the BBC's people focus, this communication aspect was merged with the main staff survey. In his book *Inside Story*, BBC director general 2000–04 Greg Dyke wrote: 'The results of the survey painted a bleak picture of our internal culture.' This was one reason behind his launch of a major culture change programme. Greg noted: 'People began to see the difference and this was reflected in the results of our next staff survey.'

Since then there have been major changes at the BBC, not least the cost pressures of a limited TV licence. The research approach itself has developed and updated in line with those influences. Like other organizations, the move was away from satisfaction to engagement, and work to define what engagement means specifically at the BBC for staff in the various functions is being fed into the development of their next survey.

In some places, an exciting, innovative approach can stimulate thinking. Use your imagination to capture interest and energy. If you have asked the senior management team to predict some of the questions this can form part of the feedback (do use a combined figure otherwise individual members may be embarrassed at how far they are from the workforce reality).

Rather than you as the presenter telling the story, why not have some employees read out the quotes from their colleagues, perhaps make the presentation themselves – or is that a step too far?

Look for other ways to group your people. In Figure 11.7 employees have been segmented into five categories by using the responses to two questions about organizational advocacy: a great employer and a great business. Those who rated both highly form the engaged, enthusiastic and energetic segment group. To make it even more personal, a character could be described for each based on the main characteristics of that group: 'Alice, aged 25, joined three years ago. She is enthusiastic and engaged with her work and welcomes more opportunity to contribute. Her only moans are that she would like a clearer path to progress and better performance feedback from her manager.'

FIGURE 11.7   Segmenting employees using responses to two questions

These are just a few thoughts. Not 'surprising' enough? Over to you and your team to come up with some original and creative ways to get your messages over.

Remember

- Take time to consider how to tell the story, simply and succinctly and look for the main story points for senior management.
- Gain deeper insights by analysing the data in a range of ways.
- Look for interesting ways to present the data instead of pages of charts.
- Surprise your audience – but not too much!

An international perspective   12

W hat of engagement and communication research in the world's most rapidly developing countries? The BRIC countries, Brazil, Russia, India and China, are judged to be at a similar stage of growing economic development. The term was coined by Jim O'Neill of Goldman Sachs, whose firm suggests these could become the four most dominant economies by the year 2050.

We put this question to members of the International Association of Business Communicators (IABC) worldwide who have given us their impressions of engagement research in their countries.

China

The world's fastest growing major economy and most populous, China became the world's second-largest economy, after the USA, in 2012. Due to different political systems and cultural backgrounds, the human resources area is very different from other countries.

However, in line with its growth, there have been many changes since the economic reforms of 1978 and 2004 saw China's first human resources development report. Developments in this area have seen training programmes intended to cultivate talent to help industry grow. Despite these initiatives the BlessingWhite Employee Engagement Report found that Chinese workers had the lowest engagement levels worldwide. Employee job satisfaction is most closely linked with career development and training while lack of training is the top reason for leaving their organization, especially for the younger workers. However, on the plus side, BlessingWhite's latest findings indicate a significant increase in engagement in China.

As part of the development of human resources and communication, employee engagement research is also developing, although relatively few companies run formal engagement initiatives. This may be influenced by the Chinese culture where the strong sense of family and patriarchy carries over into the workplace. As this is less in the larger global corporations, the culture is more aligned with a global Western approach.

One such example is China Telecom where employee engagement is strong – the company has been ranked as the best-managed company in Asia for the second year running. Its Annual Report says that it carries out regular employee surveys 'to understand their views and ensure their problems be reasonably solved or responded to... thus promoting harmonious and stable corporate employee relations. Other methods of dialogue have been introduced here including face-to-face forum series, personal visits and an Online Petition Room.'

India

The second largest growing economy is India, home of an increasing number of respected and authoritative human resource management academics and authors. The country has a long history in this field. The world's first management book is said to be *Arlhashastra*, written in India five millennia ago. This covered aspects of human resource practices such as the management of people in Ancient India as well as principles for trade and commerce.

What of employee engagement research in India today? Dr Rajeev Kumar, ABC, regional manager media in the Tata Group Corporate Affairs Department, gives us his personal views. He believes there is currently a mixed picture: 'While the trend is becoming more progressive,' he says, 'few companies have realized the significance of employee research. It is triggered in some large organizations by the challenge of retention, restructuring, engagement and integration.'

Dr Kumar thinks that some research is undertaken to improve specific scores rather than systematic cultural changes. 'There is a tendency amongst Indian managers to look at the surface rather than what underlies appearances. There is more reliance on numbers than on qualitative inputs.' Senior management is tuned to quick decision making and research findings are slower so reliance is much more on rough and ready decisions. He has also come across companies where management is afraid to address what might emerge from the research.

Some organizations take a braver stand. Using his expertise in communication and change management, Dr Kumar undertook a diagnostic research study on the human resource and communication processes at Tata Chemicals using almost 5,000 quantitative and qualitative responses in three plants. 'The research was not triggered by any crisis,' he explains, 'but by a visionary chief of HR, Mr B. Sudhakar, who wanted to identify ways of strengthening these processes and aligning them with changes in the expanding business environment.' The research unveiled findings in inter-generational dynamics relating to management, union relations, organization design, communication and leadership. These findings brought interventions to address the issues.

Such research orientation among senior management is rare. According to Mr Sudhakar: 'In India, we practice more intuitive-based decision making rather than research-based decision making.' He attributes this weakness to a lack of research orientation in MBA teaching as well as in senior management.

However, employee engagement research is growing here. 'The impact of globalization requires companies to deal with more complex data, human resources and technology,' explains Dr Kumar. 'To cope with these challenges, more research is needed.'

This view is echoed by Bish Mukherjee, ABC, president of PR firm Misha Network. 'In the 21st century employers are inclined to use research data like never before,' believes Bish. However, the reluctance to allocate budget for research is proverbial amongst senior management here. They think that available research data should be used without embarking on exclusive research for their company.

This view is being challenged by new-generation professionally qualified communicators taking on leadership in multi-national corporations with newly opened branches in India. With the entry of many professional bodies that believe in the value of research, the scene is likely to change for the better, and, hopefully, in the not too distant future. 'I, for one,' says Bish, 'would love to see more measurement of engagement, communication and PR activities to pin them to the organization's bottom-line.'

Brazil

'Employee surveys are becoming increasingly common in Brazilian companies of all sizes and lines of business,' reports Paulo Soares, ABC, corporate communications general manager at Vale, the second-largest mining company in the world with headquarters in Brazil and 126,000 employees and contractors worldwide. Vale has carried out surveys since 2002 with employees in Brazil and abroad in a wide variety of roles such as mining engineers, train drivers and technicians.

As the workforce is so crucial in the success or failure of organizations, understanding their characteristics, needs, desires, expectations and complaints has become a vital issue for senior leaders in Brazil. An organization's reputation is made up of the perceptions of its stakeholders, including its employees. In Brazil this situation is no different. Together with human resources and communications, senior managers develop and frequently use survey methodologies applied to the workplace.

However, as elsewhere in the world, the challenge is to develop effective action plans as a result. Describing the situation in Brazil generally, Paulo says that the increase in the number of internal surveys is not directly related to their quality or to the actions taken based on their results. Conducting internal surveys is seemingly simple; the challenge lies in making a strategic use of the results. In this respect, many Brazilian companies still have a good way to go. This inertia can generate a negative perception in the workforce that little is changed or improved as a result of the surveys. Paulo adds: 'So we still need to improve a lot in terms of the practical use of the results of these surveys, their constant monitoring and in particular in terms of the changes that organizations and their leadership are willing to make based on the results obtained.'

Russia

Julia Stonogina, general director, BIG Communications agency and Boris Lipatov, vice-president, IABC/Russia, report that in Russia so far only market giants test their people for engagement. Those companies can be divided into two groups: ones with the corporate management system (so the research of engagement is a part of their corporate procedures) and others with a strong owner who believes in employee engagement. However, having conducted people research, management is sometimes not ready for the changes following it.

'In most Russian companies top managers believe they can detect the employees' present mood by eye,' explains Julia. 'Other reasons for not conducting such research given by companies are insufficient budget or that the results will not be worth the time and energy of the employees.'

Thus engagement and communication research remains an occasional activity carried out by the outside consultants. Middle- and small-size companies are now showing interest in their people's loyalty and engagement too. So far they only carry out themselves some simpler tests or inquiries; often included in research on corporate culture or company's social policy.

Major organizations such as ROSATOM, the State Atomic Energy Corporation that has more than 250 enterprises and scientific institutions, including all civil nuclear companies of Russia, and the international finance group VTB Bank have recently conducted employee engagement research – a sign of the growing importance of the surveys among employees in Russia.

Nigeria

In the next tier of rapidly developing counties is Nigeria, the most populous country in Africa. A major company here is Nigeria LNG, which was formed in 1989 to harness the country's vast natural gas resources. It also provides shipping services to an ever-expanding list of worldwide ports. Its clear mission statement includes the commitment to 'provide for our staff an exciting and fulfilling place to work to develop their potential.'

As part of that commitment, NLNG took part in an industry-wide employee survey every two years over the past 12 years to establish a baseline and external comparisons on key parameters such as productivity, leadership and remuneration. However, as from 2012, the company has carried out a survey specifically designed for its needs, as learning manager at Nigeria LNG, Adesu Atanda, explains: 'The results of this survey have led to work–life balance programmes and also to the creation of a leadership academy to address the issues raised.'

NLNG is one of the upstream oil and gas industries plus other multinationals carrying our regular research among their people, as Adesu reports: 'Questions typically look at employees' perceptions of their organization and alignment with core values and organizational processes.' Industries like this are leading the field in Nigeria where Adesu notes a growing trend in these types of survey to measure employee engagement.

Although in many organizations employees feel free to air their views openly, in others some employees may fear reprisal and tend to be cautious. This means that sometimes the results tend to be at the median, says Adesu, but she believes that the situation is improving over time. The most frustrating challenge is when employees see no concrete actions taken to address their issues, but she points out that this is not always possible: 'Sometimes management cannot resolve an issue, for example, organizational structure. Management is not going to create layers just to provide promotion opportunities for employees... however, here continuous dialogue and enlightenment sessions provide explanations and create understanding.'

Remember

- Engagement and communication research is at different stages in different countries.
- Whatever the stage – early days or an integral part of business life – interest is growing in making best use of internal research.
- Information about the linkage between an organization's success and its workforce needs to be shared with senior management to help convince them of the value of listening to employee views and acting on the findings.

Conversation 6
Now multi-cultural replaces international: **Barbara Gibson**, intercultural communication consultant

As organizations become ever more global in their outlook and workforce, research among their people needs to take this diversity into account. However, it is not just a matter of labelling a survey 'international' and translating the questions, as Barbara Gibson, Adjunct Professor for Global Management, Hult International Business School, points out:

> It's more relevant to think about multi-culturalism than just international or global, with the growing mobility of employees, one organization in one single country may well have a multi-cultural workforce as well as those which span the world with numerous sites. Even if they are not located in the same place, online communication links people from many cultures and backgrounds.

All of this needs to be taken into account – it is not just a question of different languages but different customs and cultures that can also be multi-faceted. Barbara explains: 'In addition to the organization's own brand and identity, there will be cultures by industry, nation, country, region and religion – all of these can impact on research.'

There's no right or wrong – but different ways of looking at the world where people may react differently. In some cultures the old command and control environment still holds sway where critical feedback could be resented and rejected. In such circumstances, people may be less likely to raise issues and concerns. 'Other cultures tend to avoid confrontation and tell you what they think you want to hear rather than their true view,' says Barbara. Hierarchy and respect for those in authority may also influence responses, while there are different ways of working – in broad terms the West tends to favour individualism while the Eastern approach tends towards collectivism.

One example given by Barbara shows how the same actions can have completely opposite interpretations: 'Different cultures have different ethics. In some countries the giving of lavish gifts is an integral part of business dealings. In others this is viewed as bribery and corruption – the same action but diametrically conflicting understanding.'

All of these factors are challenges for multi-cultural research – is there a way to overcome these potential obstacles to get an accurate overall picture of the organization?

Barbara believes there are solutions – and these depend on being open-minded and flexible: 'One standard questionnaire sent out from Head Office may not work; the value of consistency – all the questions being the same – is lost if they are answered in different ways.' So it seems the time of one worldwide questionnaire with the only acknowledgement to multi-culturalism being translations into another language may be over.

'Surely the most important thing is to gain a more accurate picture even if that means changing or even leaving out some questions,' Barbara suggests. 'It's vital to test the questionnaire with groups of employees in each country and/or among each culture where there may be differences.' This identifies those questions that do not work well and may produce misleading information. In a country such as Germany, the works council would expect to be involved, so local employee laws and policies also need to be taken into account.

Of course it is not just the questionnaire but also how the findings are interpreted. Here Barbara counsels getting advice from consultants with experience in those cultures or involving local colleagues more closely. 'There is little point in comparing the results from the different countries/cultures,' she says, 'and more valuable to look at each set of results in context and change over time within those results.'

What advice would she give those embarking on research where people come from different cultures and countries? 'Just be very aware that one approach cannot cover all, find out more from organizations like the Society for Intercultural Education Training and Research – and, above all, be open-minded.'

Making the business case

13

This chapter shows how to demonstrate value to the 'bottom line' through the growing body of evidence and ways to link with your own organizational metrics.

Throughout this book we have talked about linking research and measurement with business and attributes that bring organizational success. The proverbial pot at the end of the rainbow is to find evidence that good communication, HR practices, change management, CSR initiatives and so on have an impact on the business – the 'bottom line' – and one we can measure.

The first evidence that identified such a link was the Sears model, publicized by the *Harvard Business Review* in 1998.

> It is no longer news that over the past five years, Sears, Roebuck and Co has radically changed the way it does business and dramatically improved its financial results. But the now-famous Sears turnaround was more than a strategic and financial break with the past. It was a radical change in the logic and culture of the company, based on a new business model – not so much 'the softer side of Sears' as the softer side of measurement. Led by CEO Arthur Martinez, a group of more than 100 top-level Sears executives spent three years rebuilding the company around its customers. In rethinking what Sears was and what it wanted to become, these managers developed a business model of the company – the employee–customer–profit model – and an accompanying measurement system that tracks success from management behaviour through employee attitudes to customer satisfaction and financial performance.
>
> *Harvard Business Review*, January 1998, Vol 76, No1

This had a major effect upon thinking about making the business base for human resource and communication, especially as the *Harvard Business Review* was well respected in management circles. However, it did mean a sudden rush of requests from organizations that wanted to 'do a Sears model'. An explanation of the timescale and metrics needed to do this usually ended that ambition. Nevertheless, the concept proved to be groundbreaking and

FIGURE 13.1   The employer–customer–profit chain at Sears

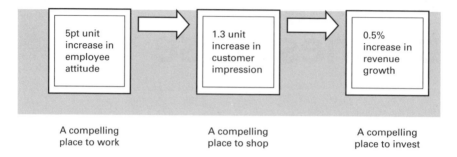

| 5pt unit increase in employee attitude | → | 1.3 unit increase in customer impression | → | 0.5% increase in revenue growth |

A compelling place to work   A compelling place to shop   A compelling place to invest

focused minds on finding clear links between communication, HR and other activities with business success.

CASE STUDY 10   Rentokil Initial: performance links with engagement

If HR professionals and communicators had one wish it would usually be the ability to link their work with the business bottom line and prove its worth to their organization. There are ostriches with their heads in the sand who assert this is impossible, but others are more adventurous who are brave enough to take on the challenge – even if it risks a negative outcome.

At Rentokil Initial, director of corporate communications Malcolm Padley had been impressed with the Sears model that showed the link between employee engagement, customer service and profitability. So when a new strategy was put in place four years ago that aimed for both growth and a reputation for excellence in customer care, he wanted to see if a similar correlation could be found between his organization's performance and employee engagement.

As a people-based service organization, Rentokil Initial's service and business results depend on how engaged their employees feel. With a diverse and mobile workforce of 66,000, based in 60 countries in a variety of roles from school catering and horticulture to parcel delivery and pest control this was a challenge. The Your Voice Counts employee survey had successfully pinpointed areas for improvement, but now clear connections were sought between survey responses and business performance.

'So I asked Hay Group Insight, which conducts our surveys, if that might be possible,' he said. 'I realized that this might not be easy, but was prepared to be convinced if the evidence was there.' The first stage was to identify the relevant data and three sets were chosen: Rentokil Initial's KPIs for financial measures (including gross margin and revenue growth); employee data (such as retention statistics for sales and service people); and customer data (around service quality and customer retention).

Hay linked the 2009 survey data to 15 months of KPIs through statistical analysis to find correlations, which also came up with the answer for how long improvements took to have an effect – there was a minimum of a six-month lag in the relationship between the survey results and KPIs. Gap analysis was also used to look at the top- and bottom-performing business units to pinpoint the biggest opinion gaps. 'I was struck with the strength of the correlations,' said Malcolm, 'that also impressed the senior management with the evidence of the financial impact of changes in survey scores.'

This enabled the organization to identify where it would get most return on investment. Enablement – the Hay term for removing the barriers to getting the job done – was clearly linked to retention, gross margin and health and safety and thus a strong predictor of performance. Analysis brought some telling statistics: teams with top-quartile gross margins have higher levels of enablement (+eight per cent) than bottom-quartile teams, while engagement was five per cent higher.

This also translated into financial terms where the calculation was that for every percentage point that employees felt enabled, gross margin would rise by 0.5 per cent.

A particular issue in an organization with such a mobile and remote workforce was retention – especially as the cost of replacing an employee was calculated at 1.5 to 2 times the annual salary. So the finding that one percentage-point improvement in enablement improves retention by 0.45 per cent showed a quantifiable impact here.

A key priority in all parts of Rentokil Initial is health and safety, most importantly for the well-being of employees but also to avoid lost time and high insurance rates. Here the Hay Group study revealed that engagement had a direct impact on health and safety levels as business units with poorer safety records were significantly less engaged.

Recognition and feeling valued are integral to engagement and, as with most organizations, this was an area that employees felt was lacking. 'We put in a whole series of recognition systems, both informal and formal,' Malcolm explained, 'such as the Extra Mile awards to acknowledge those who put in the additional effort. After two years we saw a 5 per cent rise in our recognition ratings and improvements in our customer service levels.'

As he points out, there are now clear levers for achieving higher margins, lower employee turnover and better health and safety performance. And senior leaders can now see firm evidence that listening to their people via Your Voice Counts has value for high business performance.

Public sector and not-for-profit bodies also need to demonstrate the benefits that their work generates and want to define the worth of internal activities and need to seek measures other than profitability or financial turnover. Terms such as value for money, cost effectiveness, added value or public value are increasingly used.

What specific measures can be found?

- First make use of the extensive research already undertaken to prove the links with value to the business, whether financial or non-financial. Many research firms such as Gallup, Towers Watson and organizations such as Standard Chartered Bank, Sainsbury's and the Civil Service have found links between employees and business success.

- Be inventive about finding relevant organizational metrics against which to measure the so-called 'soft' aspects.
- Identify specifics that can be measured before and after implementation.

Extensive research links with the business

There is now a wealth of material to prove this point. Make best use of the research to communicate to management. Although there are enthusiastic CEOs and boards who 'get it', there are still senior management out there who do not understand the links between their business and their people. So it is vital to get this message over with practical examples to prove the point.

One such study comes from the International Association of Business Communicators (IABC), which sought links between business success and internal communication: the research revealed that these four main communication themes correlate with a successful business:

- Clarity of purpose/direction.
- Effective interfaces (interactive relationships).
- Effective information (sharing best practice).
- Leadership communication.

Other studies have shown links with other intangibles such as engagement and corporate social responsibility. Here are just a few examples:

- 'There is one key to a profitable and stable organization during a boom or bust economy: employee morale.' These are the words of the CEO of South West Airlines, which has gained a reputation for having a great employer brand. This budget airline is one of the best examples of where attention to its employees has not only won a place as one of the US top employers but also the highest profitability and customer service.
- The approach can work for small companies too. Stamco Timber, a small UK company, launched a community programme that also involved employees in local activities. After two years, employee turnover had dropped from plus 20 per cent to under five per cent while sales also increased substantially.
- Analysis of research across 200 organizations shows that moving a workforce of 10,000 employees from low to high engagement can have a £21 million impact on the bottom line (DDI 'Employee Engagement', 2007).
- Eighty-four per cent of highly engaged public sector workers in the UK believe they can have an impact on the quality of the

organization's work – nearly three times the number of disengaged workers who say the same (Towers Perrin, 2007).

- Engaged employees in the UK take an average of 2.69 sick days per year; the disengaged take 6.19, according to Gallup, while the CBI reports that sickness absence costs the UK economy £13.4bn a year.
- Seventy per cent of engaged employees indicate they have a good understanding of how to meet customer needs; only 17 per cent of non-engaged employees say the same (Right Management, 2006).
- Engaged employees are 87 per cent less likely to leave the organization than the disengaged. The cost of high turnover among disengaged employees is significant; some estimates put the cost of replacing each employee at equal to annual salary (Corporate Leadership Council).
- T-Mobile in the USA experienced low customer-satisfaction scores. Following the introduction of a rewards and recognition programme among employees those customer scores rose to one of the highest in the business.
- High-performing companies have formal communication strategies (51 per cent vs 40 per cent low performers) while their workforce has a better understanding of organizational strategy (77 per cent vs 57 per cent) (IABC).

This is powerful information to share with senior management. A major input to the growing body of research linking engagement with business metrics is the MacLeod report, *Engaging for Success: enhancing performance through employee engagement*. David MacLeod and Nita Clarke were commissioned by the Department for Business (BIS) to take an in-depth look at employee engagement and report on its potential benefits for companies, organizations and individual employees. This collects evidence from a range of studies and David MacLeod comments: 'We hope this report will set out a compelling case to encourage more companies and organizations to adopt engagement approaches. We believe the evidence we cite of a positive correlation between an engaged workforce and improving performance is convincing.' The report is meant to be publicized and used as extensively as possible and if you have not already seen it, take a look and pass its messages on to your management.

The report found the same four enablers/drivers as critical to employee engagement:

- **Leadership**, which provides a strong strategic narrative that gives a clear story of the organization's vision, its purpose and how each individual can contribute to that purpose.
- **Managers**, who are at the heart of the organizational culture, empowering their staff rather than exerting control.
- **Voice of the employee**, where listening and responding permeates the organization.
- **Integrity**, where behaviours are consistent with stated values.

Organizational metrics

To bring the message closer to home, it may be possible to identify ways of measuring some of the softer aspects against hard business metrics. However, external factors can also play their part, making the causal link very difficult to 'prove' and thus the impact is sometimes difficult to isolate. It is surprising how much information is gathered and ignored or not even sought in a systematic and effective way. So one step will be to try to rationalize the metrics of your organization: financial turnover/profitability by unit, absenteeism, accidents, customer service, employee retention and so on.

Where are those missing metrics? There will be buried measurements to dig out as various departments own research into views from many audiences, such as the city, customers, the community and other key stakeholders. Another surprise can be the way this information is jealously guarded by some departments. I even came across a case where the HR department's request for customer service results from that department was refused as it belonged to them.

There may be other measures that you discover: for instance, is there a record of rejected job offers to talented, sought-after staff that might reflect on the employer brand? Have you counted the copies of that special publication in the bin at the end of the day? If you have a suggestion scheme, how widely is it used? In the public/not-for-profit sector, 'public value' might be illustrated by the benefits of adult education classes, NHS patient experience, recycled rubbish and benefits enquiries. Geoff Mulgan's book *The Art of Public Strategy* has some good examples of potential metrics.

Take a good look; there will be others out there waiting to be recognized.

You may find some inventive ways to calculate costs to the organization. One CEO balked at the costs of a communication campaign during a period of change. Then he noticed that people seemed to be chatting at the water cooler for longer than usual, gossiping and exchanging theories about what might be happening. As a facts and figures enthusiast, he estimated that each person might spend at least five extra minutes or so in such debate. If everybody in his large workforce did this, 300 days of working time were lost each week. It did not take him long to work out that the investment in communication would soon pay for itself.

Gathering organizational metrics together may show business links with communication and HR activities. However, this may prove difficult unless there is a specific activity that can be isolated where value can be clearly calculated. The links are easier to establish where there are a number of units with reporting by metrics, such as profitability, turnover, etc. However, outside influences cannot be discounted. An excellent employee programme of communication and engagement in one unit may not show a link with profitability if a nearby outlet is discounting goods, or a link with employee turnover if jobs are offered at higher rates down the road.

So the message is to try to look for correlations if your organization has the information to do this, but beware of 'finding' links based on a rocky premise. Senior management are accustomed to taking a critical look at financial information and will spot any unsubstantiated assumptions – this will undermine rather than support your case.

Identify specific measures

What will be much easier to identify will be specific examples of where an intervention has had a measurable impact. Here, a baseline needs to be found so that any difference can be measured and a financial saving calculated. This can range from an extensive to a small-scale operation.

In one example, a retail firm found that employees were careless when taking down the reference number of items ordered in store. Goods received then had to be returned at a cost to the firm in addition to customer annoyance. A training programme was initiated to convince people of the importance of transcribing the correct information. Six months later the number of mistakes had reduced significantly – and the financial benefit could be calculated. The reduction in mistakes also had a positive impact on customer satisfaction. At the other end of the scale, a small company realized that box files were often used to put documents in storage and their bill for those boxes was relatively high. The message went out during team meetings that it was unnecessary to use these boxes for filing – again the ensuing saving was calculable.

In our next conversation Angela Sinickas, whose work in the Return on Investment field has contributed much to its understanding, explains her approach.

Remember

- Make best use of the wealth of material out there proving the link of supposedly 'soft' aspects with the 'hard' bottom line.
- Seek your own metrics but be aware that external factors may render seeming links difficult to prove.
- When undertaking a project, try to ensure that its value can be calculated and integrate that computation into your planning.

Conversation 7
Can you prove value? Yes: **Angela Sinickas**, president of Sinickas Communications

Is the value of communication to the business an intangible that is nearly impossible to measure? Not according to Angela Sinickas whose name has become synonymous with calculating return on investment (ROI). The interest in linking communication and HR initiatives came to the fore about six years ago when CEOs started to ask about finding connections with the bottom line to prove worth to the business. Management fads come and go but this one has not only stayed but is becoming ever more important. 'Once financials are on the executive's agenda, they don't forget it,' explains Angela. 'It started with the cost/benefit analysis to assess impact and then moved on to be more specific to look for return on investment.'

This can be difficult – links between employee behaviours and financial impact are often hard to identify. 'You need to go back to the data,' explains Angela. 'Surveys should include questions that link the communication to the effect they have on employee behaviours, which result in improvements in the bottom line.' These could be HR initiatives/programmes or communication channels/messages.

However, Angela points out that trying to calculate the return for an entire communication programme makes it challenging to single out the value of communication alone. 'But the trick to calculating ROI is to focus on small elements of our communications that are directly targeted at changing some measurable behaviour that has a bottom-line impact – either on increasing the organization's revenue or reducing its costs.'

Angela uses the same type of formulas for calculating ROI that companies use for other business functions, but has developed ways to isolate the impact communication has compared to other company functions. 'Focus on one initiative that contributes to a revenue or cost control goal where the saving can be clearly identified,' explains Angela. 'Work out how much could be attributable to communication either through a survey question or a pilot/control group study – it might be 100 per cent or if other organizational initiatives are involved, it may be a percentage. At the end of the initiative the saving should be clear – so it is possible to calculate the return on investment in the communication.'

Two examples are given by Angela among the many case studies she has found to prove her point, the first focusing on external communication:

> Despite a major scandal in the press about the investment banking arm of a major bank, senior management refused to talk to the media. They argued that after three weeks or so their name would disappear from the headlines. Indeed, this proved true. But the VP of Communication identified that the amount of new deposits in the consumer banking side dropped considerably every day the stories were in the news and bounced back when the coverage stopped. The next time another scandal broke out, he was able to use this information to let management know the per-day financial cost of not responding to the media to shorten the length of negative coverage.

The second example also related to lack of information – this time for a human resource issue:

> The HR department would receive hundreds of phone calls any time they announced a change in benefits. By pre-testing a new benefits change email in one day of focus groups, we were able to clarify all the unclear or missing information before the email was sent out. This revised email announcement resulted in only three phone calls – a distinct saving not only of HR time, but all the employee time usually spent talking with their peers about what the communication might have meant.

So Angela emphasizes that saving of time – and thus costs – is as important as direct financial reductions. 'Look around you,' she urges, 'where can you work out the savings with specific calculations? Ask the right questions and it is possible for you to find answers about the value of communication and HR programmes.'

PART 3
Implementation
Identify and put into action programmes to contribute to the business

Lights... Sound... Action!

14

Whether your role is to action one particular issue or to manage an organization-wide research project, this work map takes you through the action planning process with advice, activities and plans that can also be passed on to colleagues undertaking action.

This is where the real work starts. The ultimate purpose of research among employees is to make a difference through practical action and to drive high performance and, thus, organizational success. It is at this final hurdle of action planning that the process often falters and fails.

So much effort has gone into the development and management of the measurement process that this part – the bulk of the iceberg below the surface – is often seen as a 'bolt on" rather than an integral part of the process. No matter how challenging carrying out the research seemed to be, this is the hardest part of all.

Lack of perceived action undermines the research process. Disillusioned senior management, cynical line managers and apathetic employees point to the futility of their contribution and involvement in the absence of recognized improvements. Yet the answer to creating and maintaining a proactive approach to the action planning stage lies in their hands as well as with those of the individual/team managing the research.

Action can bring improvements – and here to encourage you and your colleagues are examples from four different organizations to prove that point:

- Media organization: communication here was a challenge with media people's high expectations. Rating was low so a communication quality index was formed from six key questions to track progress. Work to improve the communication network was recognized by gradually improving scores: five years later it had risen by an impressive 33 per cent.

- Public sector body: here the main issue was personal development, which encompassed performance feedback and training. This became the action focus on a number of fronts. A year later, training to do the job well had risen by 14 per cent and over three years by 24 per cent. Over the same time period, agreed personal objectives went up 27 per cent.

- Shop retailer: work pressure overall did not seem to be a problem, but analysis by store showed major differences, with some outlets having insufficient work and others too heavy a workload. Twin initiatives were set up to even out the workload and recognize personal performance. Eighteen months later, workload was no longer an issue while staff perception that their performance was rewarded was up 10 per cent.

- Airline: a good brand image attracted enthusiastic, engaged staff. However, that enthusiasm brought a thirst for stronger two-way communication. Recognizing the opportunity, this was given priority and over a period of one year the rating of information provided rose 13 per cent, while listening to employees was up eight per cent with a similar increase for managers recognizing staff successes.

So do not despair. It is possible to move opinions, attitudes, views and behaviours, albeit gradually. What is your own role in this process? If you have undertaken a small-scale internal survey – about team meetings for instance – you may be developing an action programme on your own based on your findings. Or if you have responsibility for an extensive internal research programme, you may be the prime mover in getting action up and running as a major exercise involving colleagues.

This stage must have an overall action owner. It is vital for one person to be allocated ownership for this pivotal stage. This individual will not, of course, be solely responsible for the delivery of the action, but for ensuring that the delivery does actually happen. Ownership for the various actions will be spread around the organization and this needs to be carefully managed to ensure it does not descend into chaos – the opposite of the other danger – nothing happening at all.

From my experience of many internal research projects, I have found it rare to encounter an action planning programme that combines:

- Clear accountability among management at all levels for pursuing an effective action plan.

- A comprehensive and precise planning document outlining what needs to be achieved, how this will be done, by whom, by when, targets and what will happen if these are not met.

- An Action Owner with an overview of the programme throughout the organization and the authority to manage that programme and see it through until targets are achieved.

Rare – but not impossible. Some of the case studies in this book share best practice where the action planning phase has been successfully managed as an integral part of the complete internal research programme. These success stories were approached in a systematic way with organized project management and clear outcomes. Learn from these examples and adapt the advice and suggestions here for your own circumstances and the culture within your organization. Pass on relevant sections to colleagues who may be involved in the action planning programme.

The first step is to clarify your role. This is relatively easy if this is a one-off project where responsibility for corrective action lies with you. A methodical approach and project plan should work through the development of an action plan to inform and advise improvements to that particular issue. However, if you have been the manager of the internal research programme, where does your influence and authority start and end? Some emerging issues may be unpalatable to managers, so a confident – even challenging – approach may be needed by the messenger. As engagement has military meanings, action can also denote a battle or legal prosecution. That is not the way to finish the project and lose the potential for good that the research has identified. The internal research manager, owner, facilitator, call it what you will, needs to be at strategic level for this role to work effectively. It will be especially helpful if the CEO or a senior team member becomes an enthusiast who will support and champion this phase. Read on and define your role so this can be discussed and agreed up front – above all be challenging and assertive, you know the great potential here – make sure it is used effectively.

It is an obvious point but everybody needs to recognize that the research results are a beginning and not an end. There will be a number of stages to work through as described in the following chapters.

Remember

- Lack of action will undermine the whole process.
- Take a pro-active role to ensure that effective action is planned and implemented.
- Draw up a clear plan and encourage senior management and other colleagues to sign up for action.

The six key stages

15

Translating the information from the research into relevant, comprehensible feedback and then practical action planning requires clarity.

As the planning process starts, there are six key stages to keep in mind:

- Be clear from the outset and get agreement where needed. Plan how the action phase will be achieved from day one of the project with agreed schedules and targets.

- Design and provide feedback that is easy to understand and assimilate as this is the foundation on which action plans will be based.

- Clarify accountability. Action plans will not be in one pair of hands: some may be organization-wide but others will belong to specific individuals/areas.

- Support and advise those addressing and responding to the issues raised.

- Monitor progress and assess on a regular basis with interventions where the action planning is faltering and failing.

- Clearly communicate updates to all to ensure the research process is recognized as a valuable part of working life.

Planning from the start

An action programme needs to be planned, developed and implemented. Reading this prior to starting out on the research journey will help you design and communicate at the outset the overall process to manage the results. An employee survey that is just administered and then the results locked away in a drawer will do nothing for the organization. Indeed, you may find that it works to the detriment of the management group. Employees will feel demotivated and patronized with levels of employee engagement reducing with gradually lower response rates.

So if you are breathing a sigh of relief at the end of the survey – take a deep breath – you have done the easy part. This is a message it is vital to get through to management from the start so they recognize that the investment in the research process is not over.

Clarity is everything: ask these questions:

- How will action planning be implemented?
- Who will be responsible?
- Who will be involved?
- What is the timeline?
- Is support/advice in place to help those formulating plans?
- How will progress be assessed?
- Is there a monitor to ensure the action(s) planned is put into practice?
- Will regular updates illustrate the achievements?
- How will success be measured?
- Will targets be set and assessed?

Responses to these questions are suggested here under three main stages – feedback, action and progress – but first start with the essential step of providing feedback on the results.

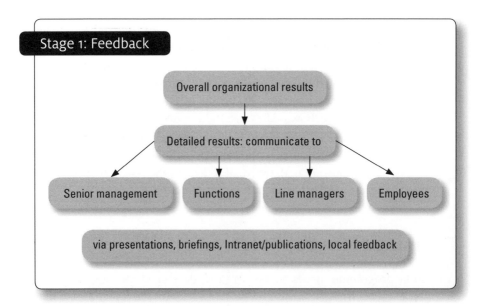

Stage 1: Feedback

Overall organizational results

Detailed results: communicate to

Senior management   Functions   Line managers   Employees

via presentations, briefings, Intranet/publications, local feedback

Effective user-friendly feedback is the essential precursor to developing an action plan for an organization-wide research programme. If the information is not presented in an appetising and accessible manner, then it is destined for the desk drawer, making action planning much harder. Out of the mass of information, we need to recognize there are a number of audiences with differing needs. Think of the feedback under five main categories:

- CEO and senior management for the overall results and insights.
- Company (if in a group), division, department, location, country (if global) for their specific results.
- Functions where findings are relevant for their specific responsibilities.
- Line managers for their own team/departmental results.
- Employees, first for the overall findings then their own team feedback, which will be of the greatest interest to them.

It is likely to be the role of the internal research owner to plan and provide the feedback at these levels. In order to pre-empt the 'they would say that wouldn't they' syndrome of excusing poor results due to external factors, think about possible influences so you are armed with that information in case anybody questions the validity of the results. Indeed, the results may have been overshadowed by specific incidents or market conditions and this should be acknowledged, although not used to avoid addressing the issues raised. You may find it useful to think of six points as suggested below.

> **Stop and think: Take a step back and jot down the context of the survey. Think through what was happening to the organization, its people and the overall market sector and business generally, good, bad and indifferent items that could have influenced these survey results.**
>
> 1
>
> 2
>
> 3
>
> 4
>
> 5
>
> 6

The CEO and senior management team are the crucial group who can make the research succeed or fail, depending on their enthusiasm and commitment. They usually expect to see the results first. A feedback presentation session could be scheduled for them as soon as possible after the results are available. Plan this in at the start of the research programme to ensure feedback to others is not held up for the senior management regular meeting. Often there is only one such presentation, but it is more productive to start with the highlights followed by an insights presentation at a later stage. This gives the opportunity for the top team to consider the first tranche of results and come back with requests for more detail about specific issues and questions. These can be incorporated into this second feedback session.

Don't get carried away with the detail: boards often get one-page information summaries and your feedback should also be in this succinct form – especially if there is no opportunity for a presentation.

If you are working with an external research organization, their team may present the results. Ensure that the internal project owner goes through this with them in a test run – the organization's own people know their senior team and the organization so this will avoid any potential gaffes. This is not to suggest undermining the independence of this valuable external perspective – just to check that terms and language used reflect the organization.

Company/division/department/location/country may have their own individual findings to consider. These could replicate the main format with relevant results and comparisons with the overall figures where appropriate. In a large group there may be several companies, each with its own history and culture. International surveys may also cover several countries and the research outcomes need to take the local environment and culture into account. Chapter 12 illustrates the considerable differences by country that need to be borne in mind to understand the context.

Function managers: again this will depend on the purpose of the research but the coverage could contain some important messages for functions such as training, administration, customer service and IT. Don't assume that your colleagues will trawl though the data to find what is relevant to them: give each function any relevant feedback and overall information but also any demographics available that will help them to focus proposed action where most needed. Be creative here – some of the relevant results may not be obvious at first glance, but will have implications for the work of the functions.

Line managers will need to see their team feedback where results are available at this level. Obviously this will depend on the topic. If the research is related to one organization-wide subject, such as the Intranet or company journal, this has to appeal to a wide audience so team-level results may not be appropriate. If there is a specific topic such as team meeting or performance feedback issues, this needs to be reported to the level where action can be taken.

Manager results need to be given in an easy to access format – if they are time-consuming and difficult to read, the feedback will be overlooked. So what is the most effective format? One organization spent a large budget providing full-colour booklets with charts, but it later transpired that these remained in desk drawers as they were overpowering. What a waste of their investment. A simple summary chart with the overall result and the team result can be effective either in the form of charts or a simple Excel spreadsheet.

XXX people survey

	TOTAL	Department A
Responses	**1105**	323
a: as an employer		
Very good	11	8
Good	37	33
Average	32	34
Poor	15	19
Very poor	4	6
Do not know/no opinion	1	0
Very good/good	**48**	**41**
b: As a business		
Very good	12	9
Good	44	39
Average	31	31
Poor	9	15
Very poor	2	3
Do not know/no opinion	2	3
Very good/good	**56**	**48**

Some external agencies provide an online results package that can be accessed by managers to look at their own feedback for their team. If the line manager is tasked with communicating the team results, a presentation template can be provided, customized for their individual feedback.

Remember that all this information will be fresh to the manager and it can be daunting for them to present onwards, especially if some of the findings are poor. At the least, briefing notes should be provided to clarify their role in the feedback and action planning process as below. Think about having a briefing session for the line managers if possible or take the opportunity of any manager meetings/training to help them. Depending on your own work responsibilities, you may want to make yourself available to assist them and/or present on their behalf.

Employees can become deeply suspicious if there is a long gap between questionnaire completion and getting feedback. After all, if they are voting for some TV reality show, the results are on the screen very quickly. So when employees see no feedback from the internal research they become disillusioned, often suspicious the results are being fiddled in some way to present a rosier picture. As discussed earlier, to consider and interpret the results is not a fast process – take people into your confidence, explaining that the views and opinions expressed deserve proper deliberation. However, it is possible to put together a short summary of the strengths and weaknesses identified in the overall results to demonstrate openness and transparency.

For all the feedback, there are five important messages to keep in mind and pass on to your colleagues:

- **Honest:** do not be tempted to be selective in what is communicated. It can appear tempting to only communicate the upside and sweep issues you would rather not face under the carpet. Unfortunately they have a way of creeping out – to the detriment of the research's credibility.

- **Speedy:** in terms of the timing of communication, sometimes managers argue that the full results should wait until an action plan has been developed to respond to the issues raised. The disadvantage of any delay in the publication of results further distances the survey and causes mistrust. In one company, managers had been given the results but there was an inordinate delay in communicating elsewhere. One disillusioned manager must have contacted the press, as some of the results appeared in a national newspaper under the headline 'the results they did not want you to see'. This you certainly do not want to see. The sooner you are able to communicate the full results the better. It will reassure your staff that the survey is taken seriously and it also keeps the interest in the process alive. Make sure that people know the schedules for the results communication – and stick to that programme.

- **Relevant:** Ensure that the results you communicate and the methods you use are relevant to the recipients. Do not produce long tables of results where the reader has to hunt to find the interesting information.

- **Leadership:** a foreword from the CEO demonstrates that the results have been seen at senior levels and this commitment gives credence that action will follow.

- **Appropriate:** make the feedback at the right level – consider your audience. An organization with professional people accustomed to detailed information may want the full data, while for a retailer with many part-time staff a brief overview may be more relevant. There must be a balance – people can be very contrary. If all the results are provided then they may say this is too much information, but a summary may be seen as hiding the full details. The best solution will be to provide a short version but also give access to the full overall results.

Make use of all the available channels in your communication processes. Post a set of the results on the Intranet as well as in a printed publication. Be innovative in how you present the results, using visuals wherever possible. However, do not let design overtake the message and certainly do not rely on a single channel to be the sole information source. Separate presentations specifically focused on the survey results may be arranged or a session at a regular briefing meeting. Keep the process front of mind in a variety of ways – mentioned at training sessions, CEO blog, and so on. It can be frustrating to hear people say they have not seen the results when you know they have been communicated – just bite your lip and try again.

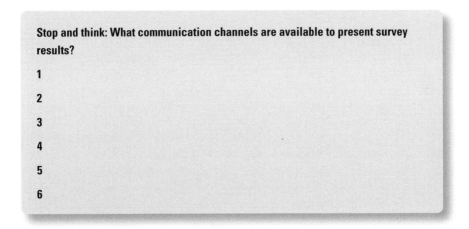

Stop and think: What communication channels are available to present survey results?

1

2

3

4

5

6

Remember

- Consider all six key steps at an early stage.
- Draw up a clear plan with responsibilities and time targets.
- The senior team must be on board for the research project to succeed.

Conversation 8
Are CEOs committed to listening to their people? Yes, says **Kevin Murray**, chairman of the Good Relations Group

So far we have heard from a wide range of people involved in communications, human resources, social media and change management. But what about that most critical group – the CEOs of the organization? What are their views about engagement, employee research and generally listening to their people? And what is their role in any planned action stemming from the survey results?

Kevin Murray had the opportunity of talking to 60 top CEOs for his book *The Language of Leaders* and found that 'leaders are making engagement itself a strategic tool in their business and they measure it, monitor it and manage it'. He notes that employees now have greater expectations of being listened to and the CEOs he interviewed now 'get the idea' and are becoming more interested in how their employees feel. They are asking: what is engagement and what does it mean for my organization? They realize that this depends on the organizational culture so any definition of their engagement needs to reflect that.

Listening was also high on their agenda and he noticed that virtually all the CEOs spontaneously mentioned their organizational surveys as an important part of that process. Kevin quotes Tom Enders, chief executive of Airbus: 'We survey staff to find out what they feel, which enables us to talk to managers about why their engagement scores are low. Many of our managers who had bad scores in the first round of our employee survey told me it gave them a real wake-up call. They hadn't realized that they simply were not spending enough time with their people, and now that they were, performance was improving.' Another measure he introduced at Airbus was to count the number of conversations managers had with their team, which helped persuade them to go out and talk as an integral part of their job.

This listening theme was echoed by Dame Barbara Stocking, chief executive of Oxfam GB, a leading UK charity set up to fight global poverty.

> We do regular staff surveys to understand how motivated employees feel, and one of our challenges at the moment is that employees don't feel our managers are listening well enough. We're looking at ways to enable our managers to go out and meet their teams and communicate better... in a volunteer organization motivation is fantastically important, and that depends on how engaged people feel and whether they feel their views are being taken into account.

These are all positive reactions from those at the top of their organizations. But we must remember that Kevin was talking to some of the most inspiring and successful leaders of high-profile global organizations. Based on his experience, what advice would Kevin give CEOs who put less value on getting feedback from their people?

'They are missing a massive trick,' he asserts, 'there's enormous value in measuring levels of employee engagement and using this measurement as a strategic tool to find ways to keep people motivated and committed to the cause.' So what advice would he offer to CEOs who might be missing that trick?

In many organizations a research programme already exists. He urges the CEO and top team to be more challenging in their expectation from that research: 'Be more demanding – ask what do we want to achieve and define what is needed to drive the business forward to better performance.' This needs to be a central part of any questionnaire or focus group discussion. Even when the CEO is committed to the concept of internal research, it is usually handed over as a project to be run elsewhere in the organization where the very issues that are crucial to business success may not be as clear as they are to the top team.

So Kevin would counsel business leaders to be more proactive in becoming involved in any research and at the very least make their expectations for the business clear to those developing the research process. 'Ask what are the big issues, what can be done in practical terms and what can we achieve as a result and how can individuals contribute?'

What barriers might be facing CEOs in creating effective engagement research? 'They need to appreciate that many of their people are not so interested in the overall vision but how things could be made better for them locally. This needs the translation at local level by the middle managers who often lack the people skills to achieve this.' So equipping the line managers with the right skills is essential, while giving more clarity on levels of decision making to avoid confusion.

In some cultures, the senior management may be afraid of the answers that the research brings. 'You have to be brave enough to take it on the chin,' says Kevin. 'But you need to be realistic – a CEO has to be able to say what is just not possible, and explain why.' The leaders interviewed were very conscious that they had to encourage the thought that leaders had to be 'bad news junkies' rather than avoiding issues. 'Getting bad news quickly was a way to improve the business, but if they wanted to keep getting that bad news they understood they should never show anyone the sharp edge of their tongue,' explained Kevin.

The CEO 'grand tour' just does not work, according to Kevin, but it is essential that leaders should get out to talk to their people. When at the end of his interviews for his book, he asked for one top point, some important messages came through for leaders:

- be visible, constantly on the road, engaging with people in an ongoing conversation;
- focus on the audience, both listening and crafting the right messages based on what you hear;
- effectively communicate your vision, values and mission;
- show your passion for what you personally believe in to inspire others.

Kevin himself is a passionate advocate of effective research among employees: 'I believe that relationship audits, in this case employee engagement audits, are a more reliable predictor of future success than past financial performance.' This being the case, he was encouraged to find that these leaders recognized that both they and their organizations needed to get better at listening: 'Sometimes, listening is the most inspiring act of all.'

Putting the action plan in place

16

Once the feedback process is in train, it is time to search though those results to identify potential action points.

Always remember that some of these action points may be driven by organization needs, others by the 'voice of the employee'. Certain findings may stand out starkly; others require deeper investigation and understanding. Part of your role is to explore the information to identify the top issues before moving on. This does not detract from the role and input of the CEO and top team. Your suggestions will be helpful but with their strategic overview, they need to review, modify, agree and drive forward the outline action plans. This needs to be one of the top items on the CEO and senior management agenda – their interest and commitment will filter down the organization to drive the action forward.

When it comes to considering and implementing action plans, it is vital to keep in mind that the feedback and responsibilities lay at all levels. Some can only be addressed by the top team in their role at corporate level. Others may be specific to the function concerned. There will also be 'local' actions undertaken at line or department level. We should not forget that the whole workforce is involved: gone are the days when the action was formulated by the managers and handed down. Employees also need to take some ownership to contribute and take responsibility for the actions and also their own individual roles, both as a team and as individuals. Remember that although the overall results are of interest to employees, it is in the findings that relate to specific work groups/teams that the greatest relevance lies. It is here that the action-orientated results will be found.

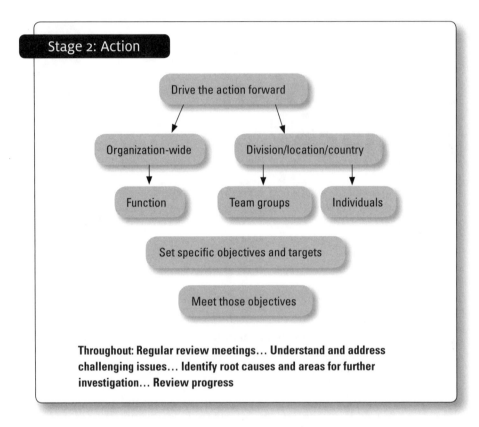

These basic questions to ask as the action-planning phase starts are not necessarily consecutive but interrelated and need to be considered at the same time.

What:

- are the firm areas to build on?
- issues stand out most strongly?
- is significantly different to previous research and/or industry averages?
- matters most to the business?
- will have maximum impact?
- are the corporate issues to be prioritized throughout the organization?

Who:

- will take responsibility:
    - the survey 'owners'?
    - project groups?
    - across the whole organization?
    - within a function?
    - within teams?
    - line/team/department managers?

How:

- will resources be made available?
- will the process be defined and monitored?
- can the process be made 'fun' and not 'boring'?
- can solutions be tested?
- can progress be measured?
- can impact be assessed?

When:

- will projects be finished:
    - is there a realistic timeline?
    - are there clear deadlines?
    - are there targets for realistic improvements, not miracles?

What are the areas for action focus?

Much of this focus should be defined as the data is turned into management information and the feedback is developed. There are four imperatives: recognize the strengths revealed; ask what implications do poor results have for the business; what emerging issues are most important to employees; and what are their root causes?

It is all too easy to forget the assets that internal research identifies and turn straight to the weaknesses to identify actions. But those strengths have the power to support and help bring improvements. List the firm foundations on which to build:

- Are the line managers a strong link in the chain?
- Is the brand reputation compelling?

- What channels are most trusted or linked with engagement? Here additional analysis may be helpful to focus action.
- What communication channels are used most by the engaged people? Here is one way to gain deeper insight and understanding of strengths by examining the combined results of two questions.

The chart below looks at the level of engagement (on the left) and communication channel usage (along the bottom.) The top-right corner shows the strength of the link between two channels and engagement – the firm foundation on which to build. This suggests that where messages are not getting through, line managers and briefing meetings will be the most effective channels. Conversely, two channels with high usage ratings that do not correlate highly with engagement and emails and posters, suggests initiatives here to better use the potential of these means of communication. Top left is the magazine – which is not highly used by engaged people – so action might be to ascertain how this could be improved or reduce investment here to use elsewhere.

Figure 16.1 The link between level of engagement and communication channel usage

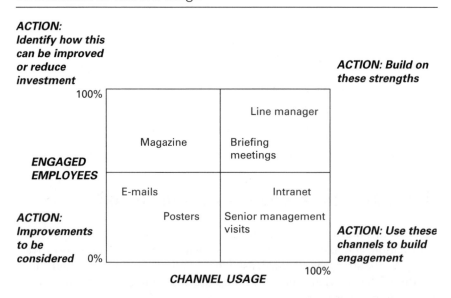

When strengths have been clearly identified, turn to the areas needing attention. Remember that these are not necessarily employee driven. If a business priority is to introduce essential change to working practices, this might be opposed by employees. It stands to reason that the action here will not be to cancel the changes but communicate the reasons and introduce HR initiatives to minimize any negative impact on the employees.

Is it possible to identify at least one 'quick win'? Action plan development is not a fast process and people become impatient for some sign that their voice has been heard. A trawl through the information may reveal an action point – or commitment to a specific action – that can be put in place quickly. This will create interest and build faith in the process.

It will also be essential to explore the root causes and reasons behind attitudes/opinions expressed. Further analysis or discussion groups may help here to explore the reasons in depth. Otherwise, suggested actions may not be addressing the real sources. If training receives a low score, on the surface the answer could appear to be to arrange more courses. However, investigation of the root causes might reveal that the training is difficult to access, not timely or relevant. Here is an example of where the individual might need to take responsibility. Is the training available but not taken up by the very people complaining it is lacking? Without weaselling out of accountability for addressing poor results, there may be occasions when a challenging question needs to go back to those who made their views known to ensure they are playing their part in resolving the issue.

Examining the root causes in one leisure company focused on one branch receiving particularly low communication scores. The manager was perplexed: team meetings were regular while the channels such as the magazine, etc were regularly received. What could the team want? He was planning to increase the number of team meetings until further conversations with staff revealed the true reason – and one it was much easier to solve. When the new brochures were launched in that area, customers received them before staff, who felt marginalized, especially when asked questions they could not yet answer. The solution there was to ensure that the team were given priority for brochure circulation. This was also a 'quick win' and easily achieved.

This is the opportunity to be realistic about setting priorities to address. A list of 100 items will never be achieved. The first step is to identify at an organization-wide level five or six attainable ambitions supported by the CEO and team. These can also be translated downwards to be relevant at each level, which will have its own feedback and responsibility for action. Thus this could range at the top from a corporate review of the organizational values to an individual determining to ask for more feedback from the line manager.

Remember

- Identify and celebrate the successes and strengths as well as addressing the issues.
- Think about potential additional analysis or focus groups if some of the findings are unclear and more insight is wanted.
- Look for a quick win to gain early recognition for the survey action programme.

Who is responsible for taking action?

17

The theoretical answer is everybody. But to be practical, as emphasized earlier, the process needs an overall driver. This is your opportunity to take the wheel and move the action planning forward.

To help with project planning, a work plan template is provided here for your use and to provide to others as part of an action plan pack. Remember, every organization differs, but there will normally be a split in issues between those that can be addressed locally by a front-line manager, those that need to be addressed by senior management – perhaps the board or executive committee – and those that will be the responsibility of the function. To manage the action planning process effectively, each level needs to take on clear responsibility for relevant issues.

FIGURE 17.1   Where responsibility for action lies

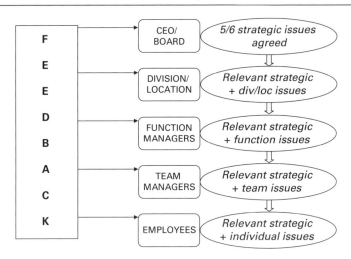

FIGURE 17.2 Action Plan Template

What are the issues?	Reasons	Action	Who is responsible?	By when?	What risks?	What signifies success?	How communicated?
1							
2							
3							
4							
5							
6							

Much of the issue of defining responsibility for resolving matters will depend on your organization's approach to empowerment and freedom to act. In some contexts, line managers have much freedom and resolve matters, while elsewhere more constraints may exist. It is becoming increasingly clear that the responsibility for action needs to be defined at different levels. Gone are the days when the senior or line manager alone shouldered the responsibility for making things better.

To start, the five/six key organization-wide areas for action need to be agreed with the CEO and senior team to show their commitment and support for the process. Some may be exclusive to the team at the top but others will need input from elsewhere. These should be passed on to division/location/country level so that any relevant issues can be translated into action areas for that level. As this action cascade progresses (see chart overleaf), there may also be specific issues relating to that group to be added to the action plan. Next, the various functions such as HR, customer service, IT, communication, etc should each have their own action plan translated from any relevant organizational issues, and those findings that refer to the work of their own department.

Think through this crucial stage very carefully so each level takes responsibility for the plans that it is within their power to action. In this way action plans can be drawn up by the relevant responsible group. Consider where the responsibilities might lie. For example, handling issues arising from the question 'My manager gives me regular performance feedback' will be a local line management issue, while HR may have a part to play in providing training/support for that part of the manager's role. However, responses relating to the strategy and vision of an organization will usually be the remit of the senior management team to clarify and communicate. There will be cases where there is joint responsibility. For example, a question such as 'I have confidence in the way top management are leading the organization' may produce a low score. Is this the responsibility of the top management team? Certainly some of the responsibility is theirs, perhaps they need to be more visible and communicate their vision for the organization more clearly and with passion. However, they cannot be everywhere, and the communication department may advise videos, webinars or a CEO blog to keep in closer touch while line managers can continue the process.

Part of the role of a line manager is to provide a link between top management and their staff, so here they can help by translating the overall strategy to local level. That assumes, of course, that they have the information themselves. A further angle to action planning is from the viewpoint of the line managers. What can help them in their role? A responsibility of top management is to ensure that line managers are equipped with the information and support they need to communicate onwards – a frequent finding is that line managers themselves are not as well-briefed as they might be to bring the corporate messages alive throughout the organization.

Stop and think: What are the top six issues that come out of your survey and indicate where you think responsibility lies for addressing/resolving them:

1   Issue.......................

Whose responsibility?......

2   Issue.......................

Whose responsibility?......

3   Issue.......................

Whose responsibility?......

4   Issue.......................

Whose responsibility?......

5   Issue.......................

Whose responsibility?......

6   Issue.......................

Whose responsibility?......

Who is driving the overall action plan forward?

Now let's turn to the five main groups we have identified who own their individual results and need to consider their role in the action planning process.

CEO and senior management team

Regardless of the organization's terminology there is always a top team, whether they are called the board, executive committee or whatever, where 'the buck stops'. This team has some special responsibilities in ensuring the survey results are turned into action. This they can do in a number of ways:

- At the very start of the process clarify their role, emphasizing their responsibilities and opportunities to emphasize their key role in the process. It would be helpful to provide examples of the linkage

between engagement/communication and business success and a
briefing note setting out expectations of their role.

- They are in the public eye so how they act as role models will be
  seen – people will note if they are seen to take interest in listening to
  the results by giving sufficient time at board meetings as well as
  subsequent communication and action planning.

- Senior people are always busy – they need to commit to ensuring the
  necessary time is allocated to meetings and briefing sessions and that
  action plans are discussed with their own staff and direct reports.

- On a regular basis they need to ask their direct reports what they are
  doing about the survey. The prospect of having to report on survey
  actions at a management meeting will prompt the busiest manager
  into action. Survey action could form part of their assessment and
  appraisal – it should be that important.

- By taking personal responsibility for certain actions, senior people
  give a huge impetus to following through actions elsewhere. By
  championing actions in a specific area, they can often kick-start
  activity.

- Help them link the survey results to key business measures, such as
  customer satisfaction, quality measures, employee turnover, and
  productivity survey information, as part of their Investors in People
  submission or to contribute to a Balanced Scorecard. In particular it is
  said that – apart from concerns about the economy and their market –
  what keeps the CEO awake at night is the challenge of attracting and
  retaining the talented people who will drive the business forward.
  Here is the perfect opportunity to stress that feedback and action
  from an employee survey will help achieve that ambition.

- The CEO and colleagues will have targets. Suggest that they set
  targets for their employee research in the same way as for other
  business aspects. Targets could be 'soft' (eg perceived improvement
  in working atmosphere or morale) or 'hard' (eg reduced
  absenteeism, improved customer care). This is another way to get
  the action planning at the top of the agenda for managers – if they
  have to report back on their action (or lack of it) and progress
  towards their target on a regular basis, this will be prioritized in
  their minds.

- One challenge that many top teams face is that of silos in their
  organization whereby cross-functional support and communication
  can be low and fail to support the organizational objectives as a
  whole, particularly relating to innovation and sharing best practice.
  By calling on the survey data that reveals these barriers, top teams
  can often kick-start the process of identifying and removing these
  silos to encourage the whole organization to pull together.

- The survey process should not be forgotten as time goes by; senior management can refer to the results in talks/presentations and other communication with staff on a continuing basis.
- Employees do not forget. Emphasize to the management that they must always deliver what is promised – if for some reason they cannot deliver, say why and when and if that is a possibility. They should not be tempted to put all the responsibility on line managers – that is an easy way out.

There are some good examples of leadership accountability for employee engagement. This is particularly strong at Boehringer Ingelheim, one of the world's 20 leading pharmaceutical organizations. Senior leadership has shown its commitment to owning the survey process by taking on a coaching role and leading by example with each member of the senior team choosing three areas to act on which are shared with their function. Progress is reported every six months with challenges faced in making improvements.

Another step in creating greater accountability here was building the survey process into managers' core job descriptions so that acting on the survey results is part of a manager's day-to-day job. Thus, not acting on survey results is seen as not living up to your core job description. To support managers in this task and share best practice at manager level, Boehringer Ingelheim uses the Insight to Action website of the Hay Group, which carries out its surveys, to provide resources for managers developing action plans and track action taken.

In the next section are some suggested briefing notes that could be helpful – of course you will need to adapt for your own circumstances/ environment but these could form the basis for your own briefings. First, you might find it useful to pass over a briefing note for the CEO and senior team to explain their role based on the points above rather than just hope they will appreciate what they need to do.

Role of the CEO and senior team – sample briefing

As leaders of the organization, senior management have a crucial role to play. You have some special responsibilities in ensuring the survey results are turned into action. This you can do in a number of ways:

1 Link the results to the business: research reveals that engaged employees are more productive and of value to the organization. In particular, a crucial part of business success is recruiting and retaining the talented people who will contribute to its achievements and growth. This information from the research guides the way to realize this aim.

2   Act as role models in all aspects of the survey including spending sufficient time in listening to and considering the results as well as their communication and the subsequent action planning. This will include ensuring the necessary time is allocated to meetings and briefing sessions to discuss action plans with your own staff and direct reports.

3   In terms of following through survey feedback, one of the very positive things you can do is to ask your direct reports what they are doing about the survey. The prospect of having to report on survey actions at a management meeting will prompt the busiest manager into action. Could senior management appraisals include an element of their performance in taking the results seriously?

4   By taking personal responsibility for certain actions, you can give a huge impetus to following through actions elsewhere. By championing actions in a specific area, you can often kick-start activity.

5   One challenge that many of you may face is that of silos in the organization whereby cross-functional support and communication can be low and fail to support the organizational objectives as a whole. By calling on the survey data you can often kick-start the process of removing these silos to drive sharing best practice and innovation.

6   Don't forget the survey information; keep it alive by referring to the results in talks/presentations and other communication with staff on a continuing basis.

7   Talk with your own team of direct reports about the results – and their proposed action – on a face-to-face basis and ensure that you and your managers act as role models through the survey process.

Division/location/country role

The guidelines above will also apply to results for companies within a group, division, location or country. The five/six key corporate points will need to be considered to gauge which are relevant to these levels. So if 'growth' is a corporate goal and the results reveal that this aim is not well understood in principle or for individual involvement, this will need to be reviewed to see what it means at this level and what specific and relevant action plans can be developed at divisional, location or country level. It will be useful to refer to the local culture and typical research findings for that area to put these results in context.

There may also be specific strengths here or issues to address so their own particular action points can be defined. It is worthwhile working with the management in these areas to help them through this process. If meeting at their location is impractical then webinars could be arranged to listen as well as to inform, with briefing notes provided.

Stop and think: What about the key business measures available which could be linked with the survey results?

1

2

3

4

5

6

Function and departmental role

This is a great opportunity for the various functions to have reliable information to help them plan action and set targets. Their role in the five or six corporate issues needs to be considered. What can that function do to contribute towards their achievement? Their results may indicate specific problems but not how these might be addressed. So here some additional discussion groups/interviews or a snap shot survey may be needed to define the root causes and potential solutions.

Frequently, much of the value of the research lies in what the findings can show these functions – but it is often not used to best advantage. So working with these functions may be another job for the internal research owner to make best use of this data so the functions appreciate the potential information that can contribute to their own goals and aims. It would be helpful for those not directly involved with the research to have their own separate report with whatever findings may be relevant to them, together with briefing notes and access to advice/support where needed.

Role of the functions/departments – sample briefing

The results of this research do not just belong to the human resource department, communications or the line managers. There will be information that can be used by various functions, for example customer service, finance, operations, information technology and facilities. This may require some 'digging in the data' but you may find some worthwhile information to help with the planning in your department. We suggest:

1 There may be some specific questions that relate to your function – rather than just look at the overall results, remember than you can also look at

those results by location, gender, service length and other demographics that might be covered.

2　Other questions may have relevance for the activities of your function/ department and you and your team may need to seek these out. For example, the results may reveal the most effective ways to communicate information – these methods can then be used by your function when communicating information.

3　There will also be other information that might be applicable – this is a rich source. It may be that the results that could be relevant to your function are puzzling and do not lead to direct action points. This would be a good time to involve the team and colleagues elsewhere in the organization to understand what lies behind these views, which would then lead to clearer solutions.

The line manager's role

The line manager is pivotal in the communication of survey results and the subsequent establishment of action plans at team level. However, there is evidence that this is often the weak link in the action chain. In view of the potential value of survey results, it is depressing that fewer than half of managers spend just two to five days a year on activities related to the annual engagement survey ('Managers: Your Strongest or Weakest Link in Driving Employee Engagement', report, Aon Hewitt research project). Jenny Merry, UK engagement practice leader at Aon Hewitt, pointed out: 'One important link that many organizations are failing to leverage is the role of the middle managers in stimulating engagement.' The report also showed that managers who reviewed their survey results and identified actions had an overall engagement score of 63 per cent vs 27 per cent for managers who had access but did not review them.

This message about managers who take action can impact on engagement needs to be passed on to managers to convince them of their role, together with a guide/support to give them confidence in understanding their results, communicating them to their teams and addressing emerging issues.

The first thing the manager needs to do is to reassure their people that they are committed to acting on the survey results. This process of communication really needs to start when the survey begins, particularly during the fieldwork period. The way in which the manager encourages staff to complete their questionnaires will have a big influence on how open staff are in their responses and how much they feel a part of participation and thus the response rate.

Then, after the survey the manager needs to communicate the results to the team. This is in addition to any company-wide communication of top-level results. To get the best from this briefing process, it needs to be interactive. The manager will need to 'unpack' the results for this specific workgroup and understand some of the issues that lie beneath the surface. Here it will be vital to celebrate any good news from the survey results so that this does not become a negative experience for the team.

Once the communication process has been completed, it is usually the manager's responsibility to support action planning and delivery through their team. A weak manager simply communicates the results and then leaves their team with no action flowing from the survey. Remember that the line manager will be a busy person and may avoid this planning stage due to time pressures or lack of confidence in facing some of the challenges thrown up by the findings. That is why they need to be convinced that this is a valuable form of management information which is another useful business metric, alongside other ways that may be measured such as customer satisfaction, profitability, quality standards and so on.

Much of the information in this book could be passed on to them to help with this task. The notes below may be useful as a briefing document. Above all, managers need to appreciate that they are not expected to come up with action plans alone – they will need the help of their team.

Role of the line manager – sample briefing

As line manager you are pivotal in the communication of survey results and the subsequent establishment of action plans. The first thing that you need to do is to ensure staff realize that the organization, and you as their manager, are committed to acting on the survey results.

This process of communication really needs to start when the survey begins and particularly during the fieldwork period.

The way in which you encourage staff to complete their questionnaires will have a big influence on how open your staff are in their responses and how much they feel a part of the action planning process.

1   One of the first things you need to do after the survey is to communicate the results to the team. This is in addition to any company-wide communication of top-level results. To get the best from this briefing process it needs to be interactive. You will need to 'unpack' the results for this specific workgroup and if satisfaction is at 56 per cent, this is a very bald figure and what needs to be done is to understand the underlying factors beneath this score. The best way to do this is to ask the employees in question what factors contributed to the rating they gave on that item.

2   Once the communication process has been completed it is your responsibility to drive action planning and delivery through the team at a

local level. It is a weak manager who simply communicates the results and then leaves their team with no action flowing from the survey.

3 Your role is key for a successful survey.

4 Ensure you make feedback swift, easy to understand and relevant for the listeners but do not use this as an excuse to conceal facts.

5 Talk your team through the results on a face-to-face basis – don't hide behind emails.

6 Involve your team in identifying potential solutions – but remember work is not necessarily a democracy, some ideas may not be feasible or practical, you need to explain this.

7 Ensure that you and your managers act as role models through the survey process. Remember, one of your roles is to represent senior management to your team – you are their local leaders.

8 Always deliver what you promise – if for some reason you cannot deliver, say why and when and whether you will be able to. It may not be easy, but do listen to the feedback you receive.

Later in this chapter are some of the frequently asked questions relating to employee surveys and the feedback process. The answers may not always be applicable to your organization's culture but should at least provide you with some helpful pointers.

Who will be involved?

Some potential action points may be self-evident while others need further input in terms of exploring the options and practical suggestions before agreeing specific action points. This process should involve people in the development of action plans to give their viewpoint, explain the background to their views and also come up with ideas and develop solutions. Perhaps one of the least productive things an organization can do with survey results is to come out with a list of actions along the lines of: 'Right, you told me what you think of things here, now this is what we are going to do to put them right.'

Equally, abandonment of responsibility: 'You've told us what you think – now what are you going to do about it?' is also not the way ahead.

So who will be involved in this stage? The five audiences identified for communication of results now need the support, advice and tools to maintain the momentum of the survey and to ensure that often-elusive action is developed and implemented. As a first step, identify an individual within each group (board, division, function, line managers) tasked with research follow-up who will play an active part in the planning programme. If at all possible, arrange a meeting to discuss the next stages and give them confidence in the process. If that is difficult to organize, perhaps an interactive webinar to cover the issues, together with a briefing pack or an online forum for action planners, would be beneficial. All this is time consuming, hence the earlier advice to organize this at the start rather than wait until results are received.

How will some of the overall and local issues be addressed? Here are some solutions that have worked well in different organizations. They are not mutually exclusive – a mix of approaches will be most productive. Ways to drive post-survey improvements through either at corporate or a more local level include:

- The CEO/senior team. Rather than pass the responsibility for action downwards, a senior action team can work successfully with a chair, who may be a board member or at least reports directly to a board member. In some instances, each senior team member 'owns' an issue, eg communication, training, etc and reports back to the main board on a regular basis.

- A Survey Action Team formed from people across the organization (or within a company, division or department) at various levels and from a range of functions. This may be a continuing responsibility for the Survey Team formed at the start of the project.

- Another approach is to create a small team to look at a specific aspect for immediate action and resolution. These one-off 'hot spot' groups are valuable to develop solutions at grass roots level and often find the responsibility and opportunity good for personal development.

- Projects: some organizations ask an individual (eg graduate trainee) to follow up action planning as a special project.

- Action groups: working with employees most closely concerned with the identified issues – for example, front-line people or line managers – to develop possible solutions and suggestions. Typically this would involve about three or four people who are given a very specific brief to address one of the significant issues from the survey. Dependent on the issue, you may want to give this group scope to resolve the issue or to come back to you with recommendations. Either way, set a target date for them to report back and ensure they have the resources to do the task properly.

- An online forum on similar lines to the action group where suggestions and comments can be posted.

- Regular webinars to share progress, best practice and success stories.

- Blogs about how this stage is being tackled – barriers and how they might be overcome.

> **Stop and think:** What are the pros and cons of these suggestions to drive the action planning process within your organizational context? Which will work best?
>
> 1
>
> 2
>
> 3
>
> 4
>
> 5
>
> 6

Where is the support and advice?

Expecting people who have never undertaken such a task to manage the process is optimistic in the extreme. I should know. As communication manager responsible for the employee survey, I blithely passed over the information to the line and function managers and continued with my day-to-day communication work. When the survey was repeated, I learned my lesson. Yes, there had been some improvement; I had certainly made use of its implications for internal communication, while the second set of results showed that certain managers had also taken the feedback as valuable management information. But the majority of the recipients had clearly continued on their way regardless. This is why I have a particular obsession with the action stage.

You need to get the message across that the commitment to invest time and money in this research indicates that this is an organization that wants to listen to the views and opinions of its staff. To conduct a survey and then stop listening will negate the value of the survey as a whole. Once again I emphasize the commitment at senior levels. Research that is enthusiastically supported and promoted by the CEO and team is considerably more effective in bringing action to drive performance than where it is plainly disregarded.

If using a briefing pack, be sure that it includes suggestions on the planning process and how to carry this out efficiently and effectively. These points can be made as follows:

- Communicate the fact that following the results briefings there will be sessions to address issues and formulate plans at appropriate levels. Those with action-planning responsibility need to organize discussion meetings to review local results and develop solutions. These briefing sessions may be linked to normal meetings such as team briefings; however it will be important to ensure that sufficient time is available.

- Prior to the meeting spend time identifying areas of the results for specific attention and to understand them more fully. These may include the following: areas of significant change (either positive or negative) from the previous survey; results that are at significant variance to others in the organization; topics where you have taken specific initiatives to improve satisfaction over the previous six to 12 months; issues where you do not understand why the results have come out as they have. Do not blind people with numbers but work with them to identify the really significant issues.

- Potential actions can be charted by assessing their cost against benefit. Those with low cost/high benefit will be priority for action while high cost/low benefit may be disregarded.

- Gain spontaneous feedback and suggestions from people but also show them a range of potential options to prompt ideas.

- Where face-to-face meetings are difficult, arrange webinars or similar online contact to work through possible solutions.

- Ask plenty of questions and invite comments on specific results. Typically, questions should be open, asking people why they think certain results came out the way they did. If the questioning is appropriately supportive, it should elucidate much more information about what lies behind the views expressed. Dependent on the organization's culture, this questioning may need to be handled quite sensitively. People will have already given their views anonymously; some may prefer to not make their comments publicly. While you cannot force them into commenting, you should point out that you cannot respond to detailed issues if you do not have more information.

- If the discussions seem inhibited, it may be more productive to ask one of the colleagues within the discussion group to facilitate the meeting. This may be the time to think about external professional facilitation that will be independent and objective as well as providing a sense of confidentiality. Experienced facilitators are versed in creating and managing productive discussions so will make a useful contribution.

- Prioritize areas for action. Factors to take into account in this prioritization process will include: What people feel is really important. What the business sees as being important. What is achievable both in the short and long term. Quick wins that can be actioned immediately.

- Prepare by considering some of the typical issues that may emerge and how they have been tackled successfully in other organizations.

How to say no – or not yet

It may seem negative to talk about 'no' at this point. However, anybody undertaking planning needs to recognize that sometimes it will be necessary to admit that an idea/suggestion is impractical – the answer will be no. Just simply giving this answer is insufficient and demotivating. Suggestions are often made because the implications are not understood. Let's take pressure for a facility such as a gym or crèche. When the details such as cost/provision of space and the actual usage are discussed with employees, they often come to understand why the initial suggestion is impractical. However, there could be another option: exploration of local facilities might result in special rates for a gym or vouchers for a crèche.

There may also be calls for major changes to the organizational direction such as stopping redundancies or location closures. This is usually not possible – but it does point to the need for a reasonable explanation. In one financial firm responses to the open question at the end revealed much resentment about the staff reductions. Talking to the HR director I discovered that an extensive supportive programme that included training opportunities was in place to advise and assist those affected to move on and find future employment. However, the firm's position was not to publicize this as it might depress the others. How wrong – a communication programme would show the survivors that their colleagues were well treated – and so would they be, should their job become redundant.

The most depressing circumstances may not be resolvable – but understanding makes a huge difference. This was brought home to me when I interviewed two people who were shortly to leave the organization due to redundancy. I expected two gloomy faces, but it was quite the reverse. The situation had been well explained to them – they in turn explained to me the reasons why their jobs no longer existed (technology had taken over) and how their firm was helping them find new jobs including developing appealing CVs.

There will be times when the message is 'not yet'. This may be realistic as there are limits to the amount of changes that can be implemented over a set time period. Here the cost/benefit matrix to get the best trade-off between inputs and outputs from the survey will be useful when defining action points.

Some possible questions – and suggested answers – for survey users for questions they may be asked.

Q. How can you be sure that the results really give a true picture?

A. When people fill in an employee survey questionnaire they usually mean what they say. Of course, there may be a few people who purposely give 'silly' answers but these are few and far between. Results are only reported when we know they are robust and reliable.

Q. My staff don't seem highly motivated to join in discussion about how things can be improved here. What can be done about this?

A. Firstly try and consider why your staff don't wish to be involved. Could it be something in the past? Consider your own style, how inviting do you objectively feel you are in gathering feedback? Point out to your staff that things will not change properly unless you can get additional feedback. Also emphasize the development opportunities of getting employees involved in action planning. Alternatively, consider having a facilitator at some of your meetings who may be able to gain feedback in a more detached manner.

Q. My department had quite a low response rate. What can I do about this?

A. For the present survey clearly it is too late to change the response rate; however, even now you can be taking some actions that may help improve response next time. Don't be tempted to believe that only the unhappy people have responded and the remainder are perfectly content. In fact, MORI research into the reasons for non-response indicates that disillusionment is the main factor in preventing participation. Thus the 'silent' group is more likely to be negative than positive. Do make sure everyone gets the feedback and is as involved as possible in the action planning that comes from the results. As the number one reason for employees not responding to surveys is that individuals do not believe anything will happen as a result of the survey – prove them wrong!

Q. I'm worried that my questionnaire or my responses will be identified.

A. It is absolutely vital to stress that the survey is completely confidential. We adhere to the guidelines of the Market Research Society not to attribute views to any individual, and not to analyse the responses of small groups of less than 10 employees. This is very important in obtaining open and honest views.

This means that we cannot provide analysis to you or your company which identifies who people are, or which show details of small groups cross-analysed (eg your gender, analysed against your grade and your department). We find that people are often concerned that this will happen (eg 'I'm the only female of this grade in my area'), but please assure employees that this is not the purpose of the research and information will never be provided at individual level.

Q. Will anything happen as a result of our feedback?

A. The whole purpose of conducting a survey is to identify action to bring improvements. We cannot promise that everything that people have said will bring action. Some points may be relatively easy to resolve, others may take longer or even be impossible. There is a commitment at senior levels to listen to and act on the results where possible – this will also depend on local managers and their teams.

Remember

- Clarify the different levels with specific responsibilities for action – otherwise nobody will be addressing this.
- Give them a clear brief with notes/support and training if needed.
- Look for ways to identify further survey information to inform any planning.
- It is not management by opinion poll – the answer may have to be no.

Translating action points into action implementation

18

Action points in themselves are not enough. How will these be achieved in practice? A vague commitment to improve communication is not getting to the heart of the matter. Each of the five or six umbrella agreed actions needs to be supported by specific tasks.

First it is worthwhile to look at the characteristics of the 'best' to see what puts them in the top category. Each year *The Sunday Times Best Companies* celebrates the best small, mid-size and big workplaces in the UK, identifying the 100 top companies in each size category. What makes them special? Looking at the characteristics of the best companies' human resource practices shows they share:

- personal growth and training emphasis;
- support and encouragement for flexible working;
- health options/support;
- clear commitment to social responsibility (charity/community).

The communication practices they share may not be new but help create the winning environment. The main themes emerging are:

- personal involvement/time/visibility of the managing director/chief executive officer;
- opportunities/encouragement for upward communication – both questions/suggestions and ideas;
- more use of new media such as blogs.

Now we look at typical issues that have been raised in other organizations with some of the ways they have been addressed during other successful internal research programmes. While every organization is different, these notes may provide suggestions and ideas that can be adapted and shared within your organization.

Lack of trust/confidence in top-management leadership. This is becoming a growing issue, in line with people's decreasing trust in major institutions and politicians. Especially in larger organizations where the top management team are not so easily visible, concern can be expressed about the quality of leadership and lack of confidence in their ability to lead the organization effectively and, as we have seen earlier, trust. The role and inspiration provided by an organization's leadership is increasing in importance. Ways that you could go about remedying these perceptions with advice to senior management include the following:

- Increased visibility through personal site visits when time is allocated to meeting 'ordinary' employees. Site visits are not helpful if they merely involve holding a management meeting at the site and there is little or no direct contact with employees. People really appreciate seeing their leaders – provided it is not a 'royal visit'.

- Developing a reputation for being interested in people – ensuring they say a simple 'hello' to people can have impact.

- Clearly and simply explaining the company strategy so that people understand the direction. Holding company conferences or road shows where decisions can be explained and employees are given the opportunity to question senior management.

- Living the values of the organization, for example by not reserving the parking place nearest to the office door! One factor that often influences confidence in leadership is the new product/services and marketing strategy of the organization. While issues from an employee survey should not drive the company strategy, new product launches, advertising campaigns and other initiatives often enhance confidence in top management. They can talk about the reasons for these positive initiatives (and sometimes their absence) and explain the advertising strategy and how the business is planning to maintain and develop revenue streams. This will have a positive impact on staff, who will feel more secure in the organization if they are confident about future business prospects and direction.

- Do also consider that apparent dissatisfaction with top-management leadership may reflect disagreement with decisions that have been taken rather than with management style. The use of the feedback process to ascertain this difference will be important.

Lack of understanding of corporate objectives and employee involvement. Despite a welter of information, employees often respond that they have relatively little knowledge about corporate objectives. This can be frustrating when an organization believes these have been clearly communicated and has made a major investment in doing so. More communication may not be the answer, however. As a first stage, why not:

- Try to distinguish between genuine lack of knowledge and a reaction caused by lack of confidence in the organizational direction. Each would be addressed in a very different way. Explain the why and how as well as the what of organizational direction.
- Use all the communication methods in the tool box and get the messages over in different ways, consistently and frequently.
- Talk to line managers/supervisors to discover whether their lack of knowledge/uncertainty is transferring to their colleagues.
- Remember this will be a slow process; senior management may have taken some time to develop objectives/vision/mission statements and then expect instant employee commitment.
- Clarify the department's role in achieving those objectives and then the individual may see more clearly how she or he can contribute. Figure 18.1 illustrates how the strategy/organizational direction can be translated at different levels, starting with the CEO giving clear leadership in defining the direction through to what this might mean at team/individual level. This template can be used for other key action points.

FIGURE 18.1   Issue: Strategy/organizational direction

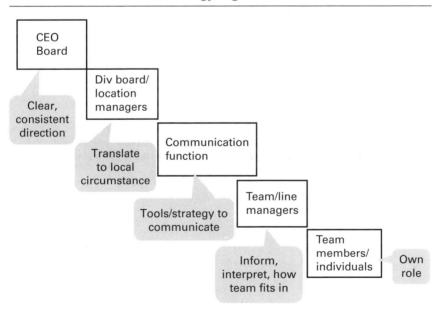

Poor communication. Even in surveys where the overall levels of engagement and other ratings are generally high, there is criticism of internal communications. Some will be genuine, although communication can be used as a channel through which general discontent about the organization can be channelled. The reasons for the view that communication is poor will need to be investigated.

- Is there information overload? Are the messages difficult to comprehend? Do employees dislike what they are hearing?
- A next step will be to review the communication network to ascertain which are working well and which are ineffective.
- Try to distinguish between perception and reality and address each in the right way.
- The answer may not be more in quantity – but less, with higher quality.

Lack of personal development/ training. A frequent finding is that people perceive a lack of training, opportunities to make best use of their skills and personal development. Ways of addressing this include clear communication to staff about the nature of training, which could often be personal development opportunities rather than courses. There is often a perception that to have been trained one should have attended a formal training course. The reality is that training can take place through any of the following:

- Reading journals, attending conferences, coaching by a manager or colleague, computer-based learning, mentoring, undertaking a secondment, standing in for a manager when they are absent, and further/higher education courses.
- Questions could also be posed about barriers that may hamper training: work pressures, line manager commitment, relevance and timeliness may be issues. It may also be useful to discuss the whole issue of personal development and the role of training in that development as part of the overall process.

Stop and think: To help you deal with training and personal development, get people to think beyond courses. Get them to list some of the ways they have participated in learning activities over the last six months.

1
2
3
4
5
6

Dissatisfaction with pay and benefits. This is the one that management usually suspects is behind dissatisfaction – but this is rarely the case. Strong enthusiasm with pay/benefits is rare; a reasonable level of contentment does exist in some organizations contrary to the assumptions of many managers. In others, however, there is significant dissatisfaction. This has been the case recently with the reduction in pension benefits, especially in the public sector. The easiest way to resolve dissatisfaction about pay and pensions may seem to be simply to increase it – but in the real world this is usually impossible. Indeed, although pay levels may top the employee importance scale for job factors, it does not feature strongly when analysing the key determinants of engagement, motivation and brand advocacy. These are ways you may tackle this issue.

- To deal effectively with the issue of pay or benefits such as pensions, the facts relating to the organization's position in the market need to be known. If pay levels are below the norm for your industry and location, do not be tempted to try and persuade your staff otherwise. They will know the market rates through their own contacts and recruitment adverts in the local press. If you are unable to pay at least the market rates you would be well advised to acknowledge this, perhaps highlighting other benefits of working for you. You may find this acknowledgement removes some dissatisfaction. If it is the case that you cannot afford to pay more for a very clear reason, be open about it and explain.

- There will of course be certain organizations where pay levels are lower than the external market and employees recognize this and are willing to accept it, such as in the charity or not-for-profit sectors. However, what may reduce satisfaction in these circumstances is perceived unfairness and inequalities within the organization itself. It is often not the level of pay, but the sense that the individual's salary is unfair compared to others that causes dissatisfaction. This is confirmed by Dan Ariely, a behavioral economist at Massachusetts Institute of Technology, in his book *Predictably Irrational: The hidden forces that shape our decisions*, which explores the varieties of nonsensical economic thinking. He points out that we value things more when we pay a higher price for them and that relativity distorts reality, so we might be earning 10 times more money than we earned for the same work a decade ago, but we're convinced that we're underpaid if the people around us are earning more.

- If you are sure your pay rates/pension arrangements are in line with similar organizations and are competitive, do not be afraid to say so. If necessary, quote the market information you have, to confirm those facts. One useful technique is to give employees a statement of all their benefits. Often the value of the total remuneration package is 20–50 per cent greater than the base salary. Few employees will realize this, so it is worth explaining the value of benefits such as a pension scheme, private health care, and profit sharing.

- For organizations where pay/benefits cannot be increased, a focus on the motivational aspects revealed through the research will be even more crucial.

Lack of inter-departmental co-operation/communication. With much focus on team performance, there can be times when staff feel that they do not get the support from other areas of the organization that they need. A typical organizational structure may contain either formal or informal silos. Lack of co-operation between these silos may be the case, or it may simply be a matter of perception. Either way, it is potentially an area for action. Ways to alleviate this include the following:

- Organize joint team meetings to discuss the areas of concern – one tip though, make sure that the management teams are as one. It would not be helpful for managers to be seen to be reinforcing the stereotype of 'us and them'.
- Arrange secondments whereby one member of a team spends time working in the other department. Allow individuals to spend a day shadowing a member of the other department so that they can gain a full understanding of what their job entails.
- Get members of each team to work together on a project to improve communications between the two departments.
- Office/factory open days where families are given an opportunity to come into the workplace.
- Brainstorming sessions to develop ideas/share best practice.
- Coverage of departments in company publications/Intranet.
- Ensure that team working is rewarded, not just promised in theory with recognition going to individuals competing on their own.
- Use online communication to communicate about the work of the department, perhaps a regular blog or videos about successes and challenges – team members can take turns to do this.
- An online information-sharing forum with best practice and innovative thinking discussed – a knowledge exchange.

Stress and lack of work/life balance. An increasing issue is that of pressure, stress and long hours of work. Legislation has restricted working hours but research suggests work/life balance is a major factor in work today, particularly in the UK. There is no easy answer. To address it:

- Focus through your appraisal system on how you recognize performance. Role models have a very important part to play. If senior managers work excessive hours, then those beneath them will perceive long hours of work as the way to progress.

The concept of work/life balance is gaining increasing prominence these days and may reflect itself in perceived pressure at work. This may not necessarily be directly linked to the actual hours of work but the style of management, relationship with line manager, etc. A sense of not being in control of the situation has been identified as one of the main causes of work pressures and stress.

- Possibly external personal problems may be a factor and the opportunity to discuss these may be appreciated.
- There could be other internal factors, such as difficulties with IT systems – for example, system crashes – or unreasonable and rapidly changing deadlines for work completion.
- Lack of understanding as to how an individual's role and contribution fit into the wider organizational context.
- A long-hours culture with subtle pressure put on those who do not wish to conform.

Sense of being undervalued. Findings may show that individuals feel undervalued by their organization. This is particularly crucial as a sense of value/respect is frequently a strong link with employee engagement. This is a hard aspect to address but you might try:

- Defining more precisely what employees mean. Is it organizational rules/regulations? Is it the way line managers treat their staff? Has major change (job roles/downsizing) caused this belief?
- Encourage feedback, both positive and constructively critical. This can be done informally or via appraisals. For some organizations an 'employee of the month' can be motivational (for others it may be anathema).
- Recognition/reward for a particular example of good work may take the form of a small gift or dinner paid for by the company.
- Examine policies/procedures to ensure that your organization is keeping up to date with best practice in HR. See whether these are consistently used by line managers.
- Trust employees: if they need time off urgently and promise to make it up, give them the opportunity to do so (this may also reduce unnecessary absenteeism).
- Say thank you. This may seem over simplistic but it is amazing how often these two simple words are forgotten.

Stop and think: Consider some of the ways that people within your organization could be recognized and valued.

1

2

3

4

5

6

When the action points have been identified and understood, there may be a further stage of consulting with other departments or sending messages back to senior management for their input/consideration. When listing the action points for implementation, categorize them in these groups:

- Actions over which we have control and can implement short term – quick wins.
- Actions over which we have control and will implement long term – slow burners.
- Actions where we need to consult others (and gain agreement) before we agree the specific action points to implement – back burner.
- Actions that are aspirations but unlikely to be tackled at the moment.

FIGURE 18.2   Risk assessment: what could stop action?

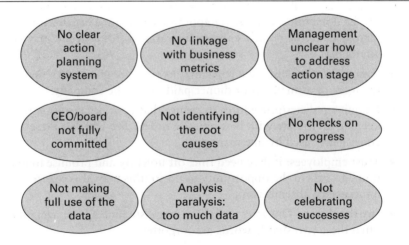

Each point will also state who is responsible and a timeline for achievement. Be very specific. Never leave it to the mythical 'someone' to do it. The timeline is vital to recognize that certain specific issues can be addressed quickly (more information on the Intranet about new projects) while others will take months, if not years (rebuilding trust).

The completed action plan should then be communicated clearly. The CEO and senior management team should communicate their priorities within a two-week timeframe to give overall direction and purpose for local teams/functions who have to work through the process and consult with others; the timing could be four to five weeks.

All this seems clear – but why is there general agreement that most internal research fails at the follow-up action stage? Take the time out to do a risk assessment to identify what might act as barriers to achievement.

By now you may be thinking there is another risk, and you would be right. If all the various areas start organizing action groups and discussions there might be little time left for the business. This is why the role of the overall action planner is so crucial. An overview of the whole process needs to ensure that not only are issues addressed, but there is not an over enthusiastic overkill and duplication – hence the emphasis on suggestions – you will need to consider which best fits the needs – and resources – of your organization.

Keeping the research alive and well

19

The overwhelming reason given by employees for not participating in employee research is the lack of subsequent action or perceived action. Thus the communication of implementation of those plans is an essential third stage of the process.

It is easy to forget to communicate what is happening even when you know the research results are being used as a valuable management tool. However, the silence that often follows the end of an employee survey is frequently taken to indicate that feedback from the workforce is being ignored.

A process needs to be put in place to gather together the action points centrally so they can be monitored. When completed, every action work template can be submitted for the record so that those undertaking action can be reminded of their commitment and outcomes can be reported back to the CEO and board as well as to employees.

This is not just about communication but also a review about the reality of action implementation. To assess this:

- set up an online forum where action points can be seen and progress monitored;
- ask for employee reactions to progress – or lack of it – at any briefings/meetings arranged;
- invite comment letters in the company publication/e-newsletters;
- arrange small discussion groups to gain feedback on progress;
- get regular updates from the action teams;
- consider a snapshot interim survey focusing on the key points;

- look for indicators of impact, which may include staff turnover, absenteeism, quality standards, participation and involvement.

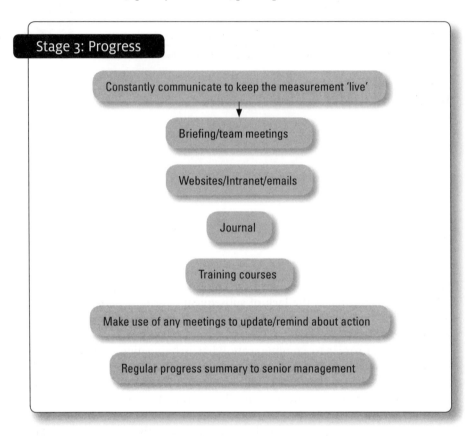

Stage 3: Progress

Constantly communicate to keep the measurement 'live'

Briefing/team meetings

Websites/Intranet/emails

Journal

Training courses

Make use of any meetings to update/remind about action

Regular progress summary to senior management

It is vital to keep the action process live. Ensure that the CEO and senior managers remember to ask about progress from time to time – interest at that level keeps those tasked with action on their toes. They need to deliver what they promise – if for some reason that becomes impossible, they need to say so openly and explain.

CASE STUDY 11 Aon: make the research work for the business to get action

Numbers are the lingua franca of the CEOs and of the boardroom, says Charles Willy. This was the reason that, when director of communication at Aon, he brought the results of past employee surveys to one of his first meetings when the new CEO joined Aon. A leading provider of risk management services, insurance and reinsurance brokerage and human capital consulting, Aon UK employed 5,000 staff in 30 offices throughout the country. 'It is far easier to get the attention of your CEO when you are talking hard facts,' explained Charles. The survey findings offered precise stakeholder analysis and gave him a very clear overview of employee opinion at an early stage.

To show a simple, direct summary measure of the findings that could be tracked easily over time, questions had been grouped to create four indices which linked with business objectives:

- Choice: attracting and retaining talent.

- Commercial: success as a business.

- Clarity: clear leadership and common purpose.

- Culture: positive behaviours.

Charles is a firm advocate of measurement but stresses that it must be firmly linked with the business to achieve real benefits through an effective action programme. 'Aon had experienced fundamental change so we wanted to establish how engaged our people were in the business and in helping the company perform better financially. We also wanted to identify actions to help support the business strategy.' To achieve this, Charles worked with the HR director to plan a series of surveys over several years and ensure leadership was committed to acting on results. Some of those results were favourable, but to raise the bar from good to excellent, at the end of the board presentation, Charles asked the direct question: 'Will results like these attract and retain unmatched talent and develop Aon into the most successful business in its field?' This focused senior management minds on committing to relevant action to attain business aims.

It was also vital that the line managers had the information to formulate their own plans, so feedback packs were developed for managers in each of the company's 16 business divisions to support them in communicating their business unit results. Next the overall results were published on the Intranet together with the explicit commitment for action from the top.

Some actions undertaken were local while others became the responsibility of Charles and his team. They were helped by the formation of an employee survey steering committee with representatives from the company who met on a regular basis and then reported progress back to the executive committee.

Aon already had the usual communication channels but, based on the survey results, Charles also introduced a blog written by the Aon CEO. 'We wanted to improve the leadership ratings: it was important to build the new CEO's brand and establish honest communication with employees,' he explains. This resulted in an impressive 10 times as many page views as all the other blogs in the global organization to prove its worth.

The blog was not used for corporate messaging, explained Charles, but to encourage honest comments and test for reactions to initiatives and plans. Employees could also debate with each other and pose questions to management from strategic to day-to-day concerns. For example, questions about fuel allowances for cars were passed on to the finance team who then posted a reply as soon as possible.

One of the messages from the research was the call for clearer information about the company direction and strategy. To address this, the Aon Forum was introduced to help people understand Aon's business strategy. The Forum comprised 36 representatives elected by their peers. The group advised senior management on how best to communicate company strategy while engaging employees. The Forum also offered consultation on all major change in the company.

'A strength shown by the survey results was our people's good relationship with their line managers so we wanted to make best use of this strong channel. Therefore we revamped our communication approach so that face-to-face became our primary channel, along with email,' Charles explains.

> However, work pressures meant the managers did not always find the time to communicate with their team and it was vital to emphasize the importance of their communication role. So we introduced mandatory one-to-one monthly meetings between employees and managers. Additionally, a communication toolkit was launched as part of a UK Knowledge Exchange designed to facilitate internal communication between colleagues, as well as leaders.

The crunch question is, of course, did this action show any benefit? Charles had a clear answer. In some cases there was a low base, but it was very encouraging to find that over three years, employees' belief in Aon as a good business increased by 23 per cent; client service by 18 per cent; trust in leadership by 16 per cent; pride in Aon by 19 per cent; while communication score went up by 20 per cent.

These clear improvements supported Charles' belief in the value of measurement to bring about positive change.

Communicate, communicate, communicate

One of the frustrations of internal research is people's perceptions that nothing is happening as a result – even when improvements are evident. Sometimes follow-up research asks about perceived action only to find that few consider this has happened. So in addition to developing and implementing action and then assessing its progress, a further imperative is to explain and inform about what is being achieved.

In one organization with everyone based on one site, senior management took the results of their regular survey very seriously. A number of key HR and communication initiatives were based on feedback from their people. Yet for several years in succession, the majority view was 'nothing has happened'. Knowing of the thought and effort that went into the post-survey work, I found this hard to understand, especially in a small company on one site where any changes were self-evident. But that was the issue – the initiatives were clear, but people did not associate them as stemming from survey feedback. A clear line of sight from survey input to associated actions was then put in place.

Dangers of changes not being associated with the research include people feeling their voice was ignored, lack of faith in the research process and management's interest in their views, and the perception that the investment in time and resources was wasted.

A communication campaign is as vital at this stage as it was at the start of the process. Some tips to help make the link between listening and acting:

- An online 'notice board' where achieved actions are publicized (and a physical notice board where online channels are less accessible).
- A celebration of success – perhaps one project selected weekly to recognize and share success.
- Note survey action points on the agenda at team meetings.
- To avoid putting 'as a result of feedback from the research ...' have a small 'survey action' logo, such as the one below, which can be used where initiatives are introduced to signify this is a result of input from the research.

FIGURE 19.1 An example of an 'action' logo

- Give recognition to those who have been involved in the action process – this could form part of their appraisal as well as recognition.
- Produce a newsletter (print or electronic) tracking action points and their effect. Include some of the difficulties encountered as well as the success stories so that problems can be recognized.
- One organization arranged an action exhibition where the various managers each had their own space to display and discuss what they were doing with staff, who were given time during the day to visit the exhibition. In large organizations this could be translated into webinars or podcasts. This is particularly useful to share best practice and ensure consistency of approach.
- Be inventive – in one factory environment a manager put up a blackboard and only wiped an issue off when the action was completed. There was only one snag – somebody was deleting items still being addressed – so do use a writing implement more permanent than chalk.

Above all, remember that the action side is equally important to, and perhaps more important than, the earlier stages. If not addressed, the evidence will be there next time research is undertaken – so be aware of this – and ensure that your colleagues are also conscious that any action impact will be measured in due course.

Remember

- There must be a clear action plan owner with confidence and authority to drive this stage through.
- A clear, agreed system and project plan is essential with work maps and briefing notes to support action planning.
- Constant communication is needed to inform people that their input has been heard and plans developed to address key issues.
- Use a template that shows the issues and how they are being addressed and resolved.

What does the future hold?

20

Some thoughts on the future direction of research among an organization's people.

Back in 2004 at an IABC conference, I suggested five possible paths forward that would influence – and improve – the future of measurement and internal research. Looking at them today, they are just as relevant with a few updates. Some organizations are already well ahead on these paths. It is disappointing that some have not progressed as quickly as hoped.

- **Specific**: the days of the general employee survey are drawing to a close, while organizations are looking to focus on specifics of their business that drive performance forward.

- **Speed**: technology has made feedback almost live so reporting no longer needs to be historic. Advances here will increase the speed of results and fast action on a regular basis.

- **Salience**: time is pressing, long lists of findings and action points are too time consuming. Identification of the priorities means that focus will be on quick wins and where action brings most impact.

- **Segmentation**: relatively little movement here – what an opportunity lost to really understand your various audiences.

- **Social**: originally I meant the growing importance of society in terms of the local community, individuals' own personal circumstances and recognition of the impact on society of aspects such as CSR. Now I add: awareness of other forms of communication and consultation such as social media.

Those were my thoughts. What do leading figures in the field predict in the future for employee engagement, change and communication research?

Stephen Welch, Hay Group

'In the last 20 years, internal research has come a long way', says Stephen Welch of Hay Group. However, he still he finds that unsophisticated organizations are using unsophisticated research techniques that haven't been used in external or customer research since the 1960s:

> But the more clever organizations let their external market research experts influence internal thinking, via techniques such as conjoint analysis, market segmentation, and dynamic questionnaires with different types of questions. Organizations are freeing themselves from standard approaches, with standard question and standard benchmarking, to approaches which help them identify the business benefits of using research to drive employee behaviour and business results.

In his experience, Hay Group is seeing more and more organizations use internal research as a business tool: identifying blockers to performance, providing line managers with clear operational data on their teams (which can be quantified into business results), and helping them to make decisions about where to invest their efforts ... and the likely return.

'For example, many organizations focus on employee engagement or internal communication channel satisfaction, as if these were somehow goals in themselves,' he points out.

> Clever and successful organizations are starting to look beyond engagement, to its connection with results and productivity (engagement is only a means to an end) and investment: return ratios on internal communication and HR investment in channels, or managerial training and development. Much in the same way as a consumer market research and insight department would in a FMCG business.

Stephen gives as an example the many organizations with high engagement scores but low performance. Their challenge is different to most: it is for the managers to understand and remove the performance blockers, organizational 'noise' and direct and harness the team's energy so it does not go to waste. Managers who focus exclusively on engagement are just creating energy, arousing passion, exciting that buzzy bee trapped in the organizational glass, when what they should really be doing is opening the window and letting employees use that energy to benefit the business, especially in a recovery.

'My prediction for the future,' he says, 'is that this trend will accelerate and that internal market research will quickly become as sophisticated as external market research.'

Patrick Kulesa, Towers Watson

At Towers Watson, Patrick Kulesa is the global research director for the organizational survey practice. His research focuses mainly on employee engagement and understanding its role in driving other measures of business performance. Towers Watson's survey practice builds on a rich heritage of nearly 40 years of research, starting with the founding of International Survey Research in 1974. Patrick envisages the future of employee research as evolving along two main avenues; both suggesting more is in store.

First, greater depth of insights. With the increased use of HRIS databases to track employee information, organizations are armed more than ever before with the ability to link together what they know about their people. This capability can lead to unique insights in areas previously unexplored. Patrick explains:

> To take just one example, understanding the opinions of employees who subsequently go on short-term disability can aid in directing workplace improvement efforts to topics that have a significant financial impact. Or, isolating high-potential employees or critical-skill groups for analysis provides targeted insights at a level not studied traditionally.

Secondly, greater depth of measurement:

> This trend takes several forms. More frequent pulse surveys provide feedback measures more often, allowing organizations to intervene quickly to address employee concerns. More sophisticated models of employee engagement are also emerging, often combining traditional measures with new topics such as employees' sense of enablement and personal well-being.

He believes that this expanded approach to employee engagement directs research to a fuller range of topics that span personal health and local resourcing as well as connection and commitment to an organization. 'More in store' equates to more value than ever from efforts to use data about employees to drive effective corporate action.

Simon Barrow, People in Business

Simon Barrow, chairman, People in Business and founder of the Market Research Society's employee research group, points out that the temptation in looking at the future is to say what one wants to see rather than what one believes will happen. 'In this case,' he says, 'I believe the pressures for change are so powerful that desires and reality have a reasonable chance of bringing the same.'

He believes that the buyers who commission employee research will become more senior and more involved as senior management realize how vital employer brand management is and put more pressure on HR to act as confident senior advisers. 'At present too many CEOs will be primarily interested in the response rate, as a low rate reflects ultimately on them as leaders of employees who do not participate as they are past the point of caring,' he says.

According to Simon, qualitative work will become more important than questionnaire-based surveys. As the percentage of highly skilled, well-educated and sophisticated employees rises so will the need to capture feelings and attitudes in more depth and more often. High-calibre people seek a conversation with people with whom they can explore subjects and where the supplementary questions can be as important as the scripted ones. There is little stimulation when completing a survey whether it is online, via email or pencil and paper as the questions are often standard with a curious global tone generated by the need to produce normative data against which to compare your own organization. 'Surveys have become too blunt an instrument,' he believes. 'I still come across standard issue surveys prior to which no custom-made qualitative work has been done.'

He foresees new insights:

> We are going to see much greater 'mining' of other communication media, which will provide important truths about personal beliefs, attitudes and experiences collected, not as formal research but as a social media by product, similarly by personal employment and recruitment apps which reveal internal and external opinions, and of course community sites like P Prune for pilots or a similar site for lawyers.

These sources are outside corporate control and at present can be dismissed as unrepresentative whingers ranting. He forecasts that measurement and classification of this data will change the way it is perceived.

Feedback is a vital part of the process. Too often feedback consists of a management summary highlighting the positives and framing the negatives as where we have some work to be done. 'That just isn't good enough for any audience let alone one with the qualities it takes to get a job today,' emphasizes Simon.

> Feedback standards will rise; employees know the reality of their work places – that is loud and clear. What they need is to be taken seriously and that means face-to-face meetings where the findings, conclusions and action can not only be communicated but discussed in an atmosphere where tough questions are welcome and not regarded as career limiting.

One final forecast is a particular interest of Simon's: the lack of any hard figures on the amount or level of employee research. He hopes that the metrics of employee research as a practice will improve: 'It could hardly be poorer than it is now. The industry bodies you would expect to have information do not know how many organizations undertake employee research, in what format and how often. This is too vital an area to be treated as a cottage industry.'

Mark Weiner, Prime Research

Turning to a global leader in strategic communication, PRIME Research, its CEO Americas, Mark Weiner, points out that communication will always be about relationships: 'What will change are the vehicles for that communication with technology advances.' It will remain of value to attract and retain talent, especially as the competition for that talent will be global. In turn this will drive up the importance of communication and engagement research among employees. Research is about motivating and gaining commitment from people and Mark believes that research is not yet fully utilized or deployed to achieve this. 'I'm constantly surprised,' he says, 'that the importance of the research is not yet fully realized. The annual survey, communication audits and net promoter scores are often relatively simple instruments given their potential to gain even better business results.'

Lou Williams, Lou Williams Companies

Author of an IABC guide to communication research, Lou Williams has long been an advocate of taking a research-based approach to public relations programmes and internal communications. Founder of The Lou Williams Companies Inc in Chicago, Lou predicts that what is going to make a difference (and be different for that matter) can be boiled down to one word: outcomes.

'Research must get closer to understanding how to measure (at a reasonable price) the ties between communication and well-defined and articulated results,' he says. 'It's not enough to be able to prognosticate or speculate or hope for the best.' Lou stresses that employee communication research is the bridge that connects management's needs, aspirations and plans with an employee's desire to work in a fulfilled and productive manner. He also points to the growing global dimension: 'For those companies that operate internationally, there is an additional overlay: the culture in which companies operate. Success will come only to those who understand and work co-operatively with cultures whether they be in Des Moines, Iowa or Bucharest, Romania or anywhere else.'

Angela Baron, CIPD

At the Chartered Institute of Personnel and Development, CIPD adviser Angela Baron is currently looking at developments in engagement. She points out that engagement is a much-researched area and there is now a wealth of evidence to prove that engaged employees perform better and hence make a greater contribution to organizational success. However, she adds: 'It is also clear that many organizations are still unclear what they actually mean by engagement and hence are measuring factors such as employee satisfaction, commitment or attitude, which is not necessarily informing strategies to raise engagement.' She adds:

> Our work at CIPD has also found that there is not enough understanding about what it is that people actually engage with. People can be actively engaged with their job but disengaged from the organization, which again has implications for how engagement is managed. There are further indicators that people may be engaged on different levels, so for example some people may be engaged at the transactional level, prepared to exhibit the behaviours associated with engagement, stay late, take on extra work, tick the right boxes on the employee survey, but do not really identify with the organization at an emotional level. Such people are more likely to leave and less likely to remain engaged through organizational turmoil or difficulties.

Looking ahead, engagement research needs to be aware of and address these different levels, both transactional and emotional, to measure engagement more accurately.

However, perhaps the biggest gap in the engagement work is around putting knowledge into practice. 'Organizations and their managers are pretty much convinced of the importance of engagement, yet they still struggle to act on that knowledge,' stresses Angela. Much of this is down to the difficulties of ensuring that managers reflect on the importance of their own behaviour and actions to engagement or because they don't have a real grasp on what engagement looks like in their context.

'As a result of this I don't think we can afford to take our foot off the accelerator in terms of driving knowledge to better manage and research engagement.' She suggests that perhaps more effort needs to be devoted to the practical education and development of managers rather than further developing the theory and definitions of engagement.

Nita Clarke, IPA and Engage for Success

Good news about the future of research into engagement and communication comes from Nita Clarke, director of the IPA and co-author of the widely praised *Engaging for Success* report. That report was not the end of the story: an Employment Engagement Taskforce has been set up, backed by Prime Minister David Cameron who gave it his full support saying, 'I am delighted that the Employment Engagement Taskforce has come together to develop practical ways to help all employers learn from the best, to break down barriers to engagement and to raise the profile of this whole agenda.'

Nita explains that the Taskforce will work with leading academics, practitioners and think tanks to progress the findings of the report and tackle key issues identified by the report such as barriers to wider adoption of engagement, how to harness engagement for innovation and maintain morale though difficult economic times. 'People are critical assets,' she says, 'they have a key role in driving business performance so it is increasingly recognized that it is vital to understand their frustrations, how to remove the barriers to better performance and work smarter.'

She believes that research tools will become more important in understanding the new employment relationship – not just as a quick fix to push up engagement scores, but for organizations to define clearly what engagement means to their individual circumstances so they understand their people's motivations and develop a culture that links them to the purpose and future success of the business.

Looking at the predictions and hopes for employee research, four main themes emerge from these comments:

- Employee engagement and communication research is growing in importance and will continue to do so with stronger involvement from senior levels.

- Deeper and wider insights will be sought both from analysis of the data and discussion groups with much to learn from external research approaches and techniques.

- Managers need to understand their own role and be given the support and confidence to understand and action their results at local level.

- There will be ever-closer links with the business as organizations realize the value of listening to their people through traditional measurement and the opportunities offered by new media as an essential ingredient for business success.

- Your organization may be among the 'stars' already putting this into effect. But if not, you may want to review and refresh your employee research programmes. A brave step but one that can bring the research closer to the business strategy and aspirations, as our last case study from John Lewis shows.

CASE STUDY 12 John Lewis Partnership: refresh, renew, re-energize

When a survey has been working well for years it is tempting to continue down the same path. At retailer John Lewis, the Partner Survey has provided useful information about people's views and opinions since 2003. The 76,500 people working here are partners who own the business rather than employees, as they have a say in how the Partnership is run, as well as an equal percentage share in profits of the leading UK businesses best known as John Lewis shops and Waitrose supermarkets.

This unique company was founded in 1929 when John Spedan Lewis gave the business to his employees. His purpose was enshrined in Principle 1, which was to balance the happiness of the partners with a successful business. Central to this principle of co-ownership is giving partners a voice and their views and opinions are sought in various ways including the annual partner survey. This is managed by the Registry Function, which supports partners, including running the democratic channels, while the survey's valued role is reflected in the 90 per cent response rate from partners.

The survey is run on traditional lines with 29 questions that fall under the three strands of Principle 1: commitments: building relationships, taking responsibility and creating real influence over working lives. The last question asks about advocacy – willingness to recommend John Lewis as a place to work, followed by an open question asking for the reasons behind that choice.

However, in the over 80 years since its birth, John Lewis is now in a very different business world, challenged by global competition and economic pressures. The partners want to face these challenges by ensuring that the successful business principle is sufficiently strong by looking for better ways of doing business. One way of achieving this is to have Key Performance Indicators as a way of setting targets, measuring productivity and commercial performance.

As part of this move, the Partner Survey is being reviewed to ensure that it continues to meet developing partnership needs and can become a KPI both at organizational and line manager level. Tasked with this is personnel strategy manager, Peter Meyler, who brings his extensive experience of employee research from the agency side to the project. 'The Commitments will continue to be central to the survey,' he explains. 'It's important that it continues to be a metric of partner opinion which reflects the cultural health of the organization, clarity of leadership and manager effectiveness. There will be no change here, but there may be more effective ways of measuring and making best use of this information.'

There are four aspects in particular that Peter is reviewing where developments could match the process closer to the business. Firstly, there is a high response rate but this is mainly paper-based as online access can be difficult in a retail environment. 'We are piloting online methods of questionnaire completion in several areas at the moment,' he explains. 'Eventually we could move towards making more use of online methods including iPads and giving partners the opportunity to complete responses on their home computers.' This would speed up the process for feeding back the results – another objective.

Secondly, recognizing that producing user-friendly results helps managers with action planning, Peter is also looking at how the results are presented and ways that managers can be given support and advice in defining and implementing action plans to bring improvements. At the moment there is no formal tracking of action taken as a result of the survey, so in the future their results could become a KPI for managers alongside other measures such as productivity and appraisals.

Third, Peter is reviewing what the concept of engagement means at John Lewis. To date, the level of engagement is judged on responses to that last question about employer advocacy. Peter looked into this in more depth by analysing the reasons given by partners for giving a high score to their advocacy, putting John Lewis in the top quartile when benchmarking with UK companies. This revealed the top two given as benefits and pay, usually more associated with satisfaction than with engagement. 'So we need to review this,' said Peter, 'to ensure what we are measuring is truly active engagement which relates to people who are involved with their work, keenly enthusiastic and feel able to contribute to the business.'

Finally, the partner survey will be re-examined in line with the current review of the Partner Personnel strategy particularly to ensure that the relationship between partners and their organization is two-way. This is already notable in how the Commitments are spelled out: the responsibilities of the Partnership towards the partners is set out as it is in many organizations; what makes this different is that the partners' responsibility to the Partnership is also defined clearly. For instance, while the Partnership promised to 'set clear goals and give support and the opportunity to achieve greater success', the partners are expected to: 'take every opportunity to achieve more, and go the extra mile for customers and other partners.'

'Measures need to be in place to quantify this two-way transaction,' Peter emphasizes. 'The relationship needs to be adult to adult – about give as well as get, and we believe this two-way exchange of value will keep us in our strong business position while staying true to the original Principle on which John Lewis was founded.'

APPENDIX

Resources and sources

To help you keep up-to-date with the latest thinking and current information, here are some useful sources that are referred to in this book together with the contact details of the organizations and individuals quoted here.

Resources

BlessingWhite
The BlessingWhite global engagement survey is published every three years. The 2011 report was completed online by nearly 11,000 workers in North America, India, Europe, South East Asia, Australia and New Zealand. They came from a range of roles from executives to front-line in organizations large and small.
www.blessingwhite.com/eee__report.asp

Effectory
The Global Employee Engagement Survey conducted by Effectory comprises Asia, Europe, North America, Brazil, Russia, India and China.
www.effectory.com

Aon Hewitt
Aon Hewitt publishes a number of reports including *Global Employee Engagement – The Latest Trends*.
www.aon.com

Towers Watson
Conducts regular Global Workforce Studies that cover over 20,000 employees in 22 markets. Today, surveys are conducted annually for over 300 companies and over 4 million employees globally.
www.towerswatson.com

Best Companies to Work For
Produces the *Sunday Times Best Companies to Work For* annually.
www.bestcompanies.co.uk

Hay Group Insight
Hay Group has partnered with FORTUNE magazine since 1997 to conduct a global survey of the world's 'Most Admired Companies' identified through over 12,000 international senior executives, outside directors and financial analysts in 30 industries.
www.haygroup.com/uk/

Other reports and valuable information:
Maritz: **www.maritzresearch.co.uk/**
Kenexa: **www.kenexa.com**
Gallup: **www.gallup.com**
Opinion Leader: **www.opinionleader.co.uk/**
ORC: **www.orc.co.uk/employee**
Engage for success: **www.engagingforsuccess.org**
Robertson Cooper: **www.robertsoncooper.com**

Sources: website contacts

Here are some of the people who shared their experience with us through the conversations and quotations in this book:

Helen Coley-Smith: **www.coleysmithconsulting.com/**
Karen Wisdom: **www.wisdomresearch.co.uk**
Marc Wright: **www.simply-communicate.com**
Sandra MacLeod: **www.echoresearch.com/**
Barbara Gibson: **barbgibson.posterous.com**
Angela Sinickas: **www.sinicom.com**
Kevin Murray: **www.bell-pottinger.co.uk**
Peter Meyler: **www.johnlewis.com**
Ray Poynter: **thefutureplace.typepad.com/home/**
Sue Derby: **www.suederby.ca**
David Zinger: **www.employeeengagement.ning.com/**
David McCandless: **www.informationisbeautiful.net/about/**
Charlie Barrett: **www.webology.biz**
Mick Upton: **www.mudesign.co.uk**
Lou Williams: **www.lcwa.com/**
Charles Willy: **peoplemakeprofits.com/**
Mark Weiner: **Prime research: www.prime-research.com**
Andy Buckley: **www.jointhedotsmr.com**
Peter Hutton: **www.brandenergyresearch.com/**

John Smythe: **www.engageforchange.com**
Gerry McGovern: **www.gerrymcgovern.com/**

Read more in these helpful books mentioned in the text:
What Are Your Staff Trying to Tell You? Revealing the best and worst practice in employee surveys, Peter Hutton, Brand Energy Research, 2009, Lulu
Drive: The surprising truth about what motivates us, Daniel H. Pink, 2011, Canongate Books
Brand for Talent, Mark Schumann, 2009, Jossey Bass
The Employer Brand, Simon Barrow and Richard Mosley, 2009, John Wiley & Sons
Employee Communication During Mergers and Acquisitions, Jenny Davenport and Simon Barrow, 2009, Gower
Information is Beautiful, David McCandless, 2010, Harper Collins
Managing Transitions, William Bridges, 2009, Nicholas Brealey
The Language of Leaders, Kevin Murray, 2012, Kogan Page
The CEO: Chief Engagement Officer, John Smythe, 2007, Gower
The Art of Public Strategy, Geoff Mulgan, 2009, Oxford University Press
Predictably Irrational: The Hidden Forces that Shape our Decisions, Dan Ariely, 2008, Harper Collins
Market Research Handbook, ESOMAR, 2007, John Wiley & Sons

Organizations

International Association of Business Communicators (IABC): **www.iabc.com**
Institute of Internal Communication (IoIC): **www.ioic.org.uk**
Market Research Society: **www.mrs.org.uk**
ESOMAR: **www.esomar.org**

Your Feedback

In the spirit of research, I would welcome your feedback about this book at: www.surveymonkey.com/s/engbook

INDEX

NB: page numbers in *italic* indicate figures or tables